JESUS *and the*

JEWISH ROOTS *of the* EUCHARIST

JESUS *and the* JEWISH ROOTS *of the* EUCHARIST

Unlocking the Secrets of the Last Supper

BRANT PITRE

Doubleday

New York   London   Toronto   Sydney   Auckland

NOTE: All scripture quotations are from the *Revised Standard Version Catholic Edition* (Toronto: Thomas Nelson & Sons, 1966). All emphasis in quotations is the author's.

Originally published in hardcover in the United States by Doubleday Religion, an imprint of the Crown Publishing Group, a division of Penguin Random House LLC, New York, in 2011.

Nihil Obstat: Monsignor Francis J. McAree, Censor Librorum
Imprimatur: Most Reverend Dennis J. Sullivan, Auxiliary Bishop and Vicar General, Archdiocese of New York

The *Nihil Obstat* and *Imprimatur* are official declarations that a book or pamphlet is free of doctrinal or moral error. No implication is contained therein that those who have granted the *Nihil Obstat* or *Imprimatur* agree with the content, opinions, or statements expressed.

Library of Congress Cataloging-in-Publication Data
Pitre, Brant James. Jesus and the Jewish roots of the Eucharist: unlocking the secrets of the Last Supper / Brant Pitre.—1st ed.
1. Lord's Supper—History. 2. Catholic Church—Relations— Judaism. 3. Judaism—Relations—Catholic Church. I. Title.
BV825.3.P58 2011
234'.163—dc22   2010024979

ISBN 978-0-385-53186-3
eBook ISBN 978-0-385-53185-6
Special Sales ISBN 978-0-525-61605-4

PRINTED IN THE UNITED STATES OF AMERICA

Cover design: Jessie Sayward Bright
Cover art: *The Last Supper* by The Perea Master © Christie's Images Ltd./SuperStock

10 9 8 7 6 5 4 3

First Paperback Edition

For Elizabeth

CONTENTS

⤜• ⤛

At our remove of two thousand years, it seems natural for us to look upon Jesus' crucifixion as a sacrifice. Christians are heirs to a long tradition of talking that way, praying that way, thinking that way. But first-century Jews who witnessed the event would not and could not have seen the crucifixion as a sacrifice. It bore none of the marks of a sacrifice in the ancient world. On Calvary there was no altar and no credentialed priest. There was indeed a death, but it took place apart from the Temple, which was the only valid place of sacrifice in Judaism, and even outside the walls of the holy city.

St. Paul, however, made the connections for his generation, and especially for his fellow Jews. In First Corinthians, after introducing the word of the cross (1:18), he calls Christ "our paschal lamb" who "has been sacrificed" (5:7). Thus he makes the connection between the Passover celebrated as the Last Supper and the crucifixion on Calvary.

Indeed, it was that first Eucharist that transformed Jesus' death from an execution to an offering. At the Last Supper he gave his body to be broken, his blood to be poured out, as if on an altar.

As Paul retold the story of the Last Supper (1 Corinthians 11:23–25), he spoke of the event in sacrificial terms. He quotes Jesus as calling it "the new covenant in my blood," an evocation of Moses' words as he made a sacrificial offering of oxen: "Behold the blood of the covenant" (Exodus 24:8). It was the sacrificial blood that ratified the covenant, because Moses said so, in the one instance, and because Jesus said so in the other.

Paul also quotes Jesus calling the Supper a "remembrance," which was another technical term for a specific type of Temple sacrifice (the memorial offering).

And just in case we missed any of those connections, Paul compares the Christian Supper (the Eucharist) with the sacrifices of the Temple (1 Corinthians 10:18) and even with pagan sacrifices (1 Corinthians 10:19–21). *All sacrifices*, he says, bring about a communion, a fellowship. The offerings of idolatry bring about a communion with demons, but the Christian sacrifice brings about a communion with the body and blood of Jesus (1 Corinthians 10:16).

Paul's vision of the Passion is stunning. He shows us that it is not merely about how much Jesus *suffered*, but how much he *loves*. Love transforms suffering into sacrifice.

The death on Calvary was not simply a brutal and bloody execution. Jesus' death had been transformed by his self-offering in the Upper Room. It had become the offering of an unblemished paschal victim, the self-offering of a high priest who gave himself for the redemption of others. He is both priest and victim. For "Christ loved us and gave himself up for us, a fragrant offering and sacrifice to God" (Ephesians 5:2). That is love: the total gift of self.

The Eucharist infuses that love into us, uniting our love with Christ's, our sacrifice with his. Saint Paul preached: "I appeal to you therefore, brethren, by the mercies of God, to present your bodies as a living sacrifice, holy and acceptable to God, which is your spiritual worship" (Romans 12:1). Note that he speaks of "bodies" in the plural, but "sacrifice" in the singular. For we are many, but our sacrifice is one with Jesus' own, which is once for all (see Hebrews 7:27, 9:12, 9:26, 10:10).

Paul teaches us that the Eucharist is ordered to the cross, and the cross is ordered to the resurrection. It is the crucified and resurrected humanity of Jesus that Christians consume in Holy Communion. We come to it by way of suffering, but we receive the Host as a pledge of lasting glory, and we have the grace to endure the rest.

This is something we cannot appreciate fully until we have learned to see it "as it was in the beginning," as it was for those first Jewish Christians, who saw an old, familiar world ending and a new one descending as a heavenly Jerusalem. This beautiful book by Dr. Brant Pitre gives us all we need for that appreciation of what was, so that we can see, ever more clearly, what "is now and ever shall be, world without end."

In the World to Come there is no eating or drinking...but the righteous sit with crowns on their heads, feasting on the brightness of the divine presence, as it says, "And they beheld God, and did eat and drink" (Exodus 24:11).

—Babylonian Talmud, Tractate *Berakoth* 17a

[The priests in the Temple] used to lift up [the golden table] and exhibit the Bread of the Presence on it to those who came up for the festivals, saying to them, "Behold, God's love for you!"

—Babylonian Talmud, Tractate *Menahoth* 29a

INTRODUCTION

❖ ❖

I will never forget that day. I was a college sophomore and engaged to be married. It was a beautiful spring morning, and my future bride and I were driving through our hometown to visit her pastor to talk about the wedding. We were as happy as could be. There was just one small problem: I was a cradle Catholic, and Elizabeth was a Southern Baptist. As a result, we had our differences of opinion over how to interpret the Bible but had come to respect each other's beliefs even where we disagreed. For this reason, we had big hopes of bringing our two families together in what we then referred to as an "ecumenical" wedding service, one that would be respectful of both families' traditions.

Since, however, a wedding can only take place in one building, the plan was to have the service at her church. So we were on our way to see her pastor to discuss the big day. Originally, we were scheduled to have only a brief meeting with him—fifteen minutes or so—in order to get his permission to celebrate the marriage there. We thought the meeting would go off without a hitch, especially since her late grandfather had been the founding pastor and built the church himself. Surely we wouldn't have any trouble getting permission to use the sanctuary.

Sadly, we were mistaken. For her church had just gotten a new pastor, one we had never met. He was newly ordained: fresh out of seminary and aflame with the fire of the Gospel. And, more important, he was none too friendly toward the Catholic Church.

At first, the tone of our meeting was polite and conversational. However, before her pastor would agree to let us have our wedding there, he wanted to find out more about our personal beliefs. At that point, the fifteen-minute meeting—which was supposed to be about getting permission to use the building—turned into a nearly *three-hour* theological wrestling match. For what seemed like an eternity, he grilled me on every single controversial point of the Catholic faith:

"Why do you Catholics worship Mary?" He fired at me, "Don't you know that God alone is to be worshiped?"

"How can you believe in Purgatory?" He said, "Show me where the word Purgatory ever occurs in the Bible! Why do you pray to the dead? Don't you know that's necromancy?"

"Did you know that the Catholic Church *added* books to the Bible in the Middle Ages?" he inquired. "What authority does a man-made institution have to change the Word of God?"

"And what about the Pope?" he asked. "Do you really believe that he, a mere man, is infallible? That he *never* sins? No one is sinless but Jesus Christ!"

And so it went, on and on—for hours. Fortunately, I was the studious type, and had the mildly illustrious honor of having won my local parish's catechism quiz-bowl. Moreover, I was an avid reader, and at age eighteen had already read through the entire Bible, cover to cover, in my freshman year. So I was able to put up something of a fight, trying to explain myself. But that only made him come on stronger, and, in the end, none of my attempts to defend my Catholic beliefs were successful.

Many things were said over the course of that meeting. But the one exchange that stands out most in my memory was when we turned to the topic of the Lord's Supper— what Catholics call the Eucharist.

In order to understand what I'm about to say, it's important to understand what the Catholic Church teaches about the Eucharist. The English word *Eucharist* comes from the Greek *eucharistia*, which means "thanksgiving," as in Jesus' act of "giving thanks" (*eucharistesas*) at the Last Supper (Matthew 26:26–28). According to the Catholic faith, when a Catholic priest takes the bread and wine of the Eucharist and says the words of Jesus from the Last Supper, "This is my body . . . This is my blood," the bread and wine actually *become* the body and blood of Christ. Although the *appearances* of bread and wine remain—the taste, the touch, etc.— the *reality* is that there is no more bread and wine. There's only Jesus: his body, his blood, his soul, and his divinity. This is called the doctrine of Jesus' "Real Presence" in the Eucharist. You can see why this might be difficult for anyone to believe, including my new theological sparring partner.

"And what about the Lord's Supper?" he said. "How can you Catholics teach that bread and wine actually become Jesus' body and blood? Do you really *believe* that? It's ridiculous!"

"Of course I believe it," I replied. "The Eucharist is the most important thing in my life."

To which he responded: "Don't you understand that if the Lord's Supper were really Jesus' body and blood, then you would be eating Jesus. That's cannibalism!" Then, pausing for dramatic effect, he said, "Don't you realize that if you were really able to eat Jesus, you would *become Jesus?*"

I had no idea what to say to that, and the knowing smile he wore showed that he knew he had me.

To be sure, I didn't know how to respond to this at the time. Even though I had read the Bible, I still hadn't memorized where every single one of my beliefs could be found in Scripture. I knew something about what I believed, but not necessarily why I believed it, much less where to find evidence for it.

As the years went by, I would eventually learn that there are dozens of books on these subjects, providing biblical answers to all of his objections. At the time, however, I had grown up in a predominantly Catholic part of southeastern Louisiana and had never had to defend myself like this before. Sure, Elizabeth and her family members had questioned me before about topics like Purgatory or why Catholic Bibles had more books in them than Protestant Bibles, but this was the first time I had ever encountered an all-out biblical assault on the Catholic faith. The pastor was relentless, and the result was disastrous. Eventually, I just clammed up, shut up, and let him rage on.

In the end, he concluded the session by turning to my future wife and saying, "I'm sorry, but I can't give you a definite answer right now. I have serious concerns about yoking you to an unbeliever."

Needless to say, Elizabeth and I left his office devastated. We rode home in tears of disbelief at what had just happened.

That night was awful.

As I tried to sleep, my mind raced as it ran through all the topics we had debated. Over and over again, I replayed the scenes in my head—wishing I had said this, regretting I had not said that. The more I thought about what had happened, the more upset I got.

And the more upset I got, the more I realized that of all my beliefs the pastor had attacked, there was one that hurt most: his mockery of the real presence of Jesus in the Eucharist. I couldn't stop thinking about it. All of my life, the Eucharist had been the center of my faith. As a child, I had no recollection of ever missing a Sunday Eucharist (what Catholics commonly call the Mass)—ever—for any reason. Moreover, I also had no recollection of ever not believing, or even doubting for a single moment, that the Eucharist was really the body and blood of Jesus. That might sound hard to believe, but it's true. I had just accepted it by faith. Even in my older years, as theological questions emerged, it had never even occurred to me that the Church's teaching on the real presence of Jesus in the Eucharist might be unbiblical, much less untrue. Yet here was a pastor with a graduate degree in theology, who clearly knew more than I did about the Bible, ridiculing the very idea of such a thing.

So, where was I to turn? What was I to do? Logically, the next step was to go back to Scripture and look for myself.

That's when something happened that would change the course of my life forever.

Getting up from my bed and turning on my lamp, I went straight to the bookshelf and picked up the leather-bound, gold-leafed New American Bible that my parents had given me as a gift for my Confirmation. I was desperate. *Is it possible,* I thought, *that the real presence of Jesus isn't scriptural?* I was determined to stay up all night if I had to and find out for myself. But when I opened that Bible, something remarkable happened. (And here I must insist that I'm telling the truth.) I didn't flip through the pages. I didn't scan the index. I didn't search for some passage that might speak to how I was feeling. I just opened up my Bible, looked down, and immediately saw these words of Jesus, written in red letters:

> *Amen, Amen, I say to you, unless you eat the flesh of the Son of Man and drink his blood, you do not have life within you.* Whoever eats my flesh and drinks my blood has eternal life, and I will raise him on the last day. *For my flesh is true food, and my blood is true drink.* (JOHN 6:53–54)

For the second time that day, my eyes were flooded with tears, so many that I could barely see the pages. This time, however, they were tears of joy—the joy of discovering that my childhood belief in the Eucharist was not quite as unbiblical as that pastor had suggested. I was elated to find that Jesus himself had said that his flesh and blood were real food and real drink, which he had commanded his disciples to receive so that they might have eternal life. *What?! I* thought. *Is this really in the Bible? How come I never saw this before? How did I miss this?*

At that moment, I have to confess, I was tempted to look up the phone number of that pastor, call him up, and ask him, "Hey, have you ever read John 6? It's all right here! Jesus himself says, 'He who *eats me* will live because of me.' Check out verse 57!"

But I didn't do that. (In fact, sad to say, I don't think I ever had another conversation with him.) I just closed my Bible, totally blown away by what I had just found. The more I thought about it, the more amazed I was. As I had already learned, the Bible is one long book. As I would later find out, only a handful of passages actually deal with the Eucharist, and only a few of those directly address the issue of Jesus' Eucharistic presence. What are the chances that that night, in the wake of that conversation, at that moment, I would open the Bible not only to a passage about the Eucharist, but to those verses? What are the odds that I would turn directly to Jesus' most explicit teaching on the reality of his Eucharistic presence in all of Scripture?

All that happened more than fifteen years ago. But it was a major turning point for me. In many ways, it's one of the reasons that today I am a biblical scholar and spend my days (and nights) studying, teaching, and writing about the Bible. In effect, my exchange with that pastor poured gasoline on the fire of my interest in Scripture. As a result, I shifted my primary major from English literature to religious studies, and continued to study the Bible, eventually earning my Ph.D. in the New Testament from the University of Notre Dame.

During those years, I learned two things that would prove important for my own journey, and for explaining why I finally decided to write this book.

First, I realized that when it comes to the words of Jesus

in the Gospels, things aren't quite so simple as they seemed at first. To say the least, not everyone sees John chapter 6 as conclusive evidence for the real presence of Jesus in the Eucharist. For one thing, many interpret Jesus' words symbolically or "spiritually," arguing that Jesus did not intend for his disciples to take him literally. "The flesh is of no avail; it is the Spirit that gives life," he says in the same chapter. "The words I have spoken to you are spirit and life" (John 6:63). In addition, some scholars argue that Jesus, as a first-century Jew, could never have said such things. The Law of Moses is very clear when it prohibits the drinking of blood: "You shall not drink the blood" (Leviticus 17:11). From this point of view, the idea of a Jewish man, even a Jewish prophet, commanding others to eat his flesh and drink his blood is historically implausible, if not impossible.

Second, at every stage of my studies—undergraduate, graduate, and doctoral—I had the privilege of being able to study under the guidance of several Jewish professors. These teachers not only opened up the world of Judaism to me, they also helped me to realize something very important about Christianity. If you really want to know who Jesus was and what he was saying and doing, then you need to interpret his words and deeds in their historical context. And that means becoming familiar with not just ancient Christianity but also with ancient Judaism. As one of my former professors, Amy-Jill Levine, writes:

> Jesus had to have made sense in his own context, and his context is that of Galilee and Judea. Jesus cannot be fully understood unless he is understood through first-century Jewish eyes and heard through first-century Jewish ears. . . . To under-

stand Jesus' impact in his own setting—why some chose to follow him, others to dismiss him, and still others to seek his death—requires an understanding of that setting.

Levine's words are paralleled in a recent book by Pope Benedict XVI, who writes:

> [I]t must be said that *the message of Jesus is completely misunderstood if it is separated from the context of the faith and hope of the Chosen People*: like John the Baptist, his direct Precursor, Jesus above all addresses Israel (cf. Mt 15:24), in order to "gather" it together in the eschatological time that arrived with him.

These are strong words. According to Pope Benedict, to the extent that you separate the words of Jesus from the faith and hope of the Jewish people, you risk "completely misunderstanding" him. As we will see in this book, this is precisely what has happened with various interpretations of Jesus' words at the Last Supper. Jesus' Jewish context has been repeatedly ignored, and as a result, many readers of the Gospels have not understood him.

In addition, I hope to show that by focusing on the Jewish context of Jesus' teachings, all of his words not only begin to make sense; they come alive in a way that is exciting and powerful. I can testify to this from experience; the more I've studied Jesus' teachings in their Jewish environment, the more he fascinates me, and the more he challenges me to change the way I see who he was, what he was doing, and what it means for my life today.

So, whether you're Catholic or Protestant, Jewish or

Gentile, believer or nonbeliever, if you've ever wondered, *Who was Jesus really?* I invite you to come along with me on this journey. As we will see, it is precisely the Jewish roots of Jesus' words that will enable us to unlock the secrets of who he was and what he meant when he said to his disciples, "Take, eat, this is my body."

1

THE MYSTERY OF THE LAST SUPPER

JESUS AND JUDAISM

Jesus of Nazareth was a Jew. He was born of a Jewish mother, received the Jewish sign of circumcision, and grew up in a Jewish town in Galilee. As a young man, he studied the Jewish Torah, celebrated Jewish feasts and holy days, and went on pilgrimages to the Jewish Temple. And, when he was thirty years old, he began to preach in the Jewish synagogues about the fulfillment of the Jewish Scriptures, proclaiming the kingdom of God to the Jewish people. At the very end of his life, he celebrated the Jewish Passover, was tried by the Jewish council of priests and elders known as the Sanhedrin, and was crucified outside the great Jewish city of Jerusalem. Above his head hung a placard that read in Greek, Latin, and Hebrew: "Jesus of Nazareth, King of the Jews" (John 19:19).

As this list demonstrates, the Jewishness of Jesus is a historical fact. But is it important? If Jesus was a real person who really lived in history, then the answer must be "Yes." To be sure, over the centuries, Christian theologians have written books about Jesus that don't spend much time studying his Jewish context. Much of the effort has gone into exploring the question of his divine identity. However, for anyone interested in exploring the humanity of Jesus—especially the original meaning of his words and actions—a focus on his Jewish identity is absolutely necessary. Jesus was a historical figure, living in a particular time and place. Therefore, any attempt to understand his words and deeds must reckon with the fact that Jesus lived in an ancient *Jewish* context. Although on a few occasions Jesus welcomed non-Jews (Gentiles) who accepted him as Messiah, he himself declared that he had been sent first and foremost "to the lost sheep of the house of Israel" (Matthew 10:5). This means that virtually all of his teachings were directed to a Jewish audience in a Jewish setting.

For instance, during his first sermon in his hometown synagogue at Nazareth, Jesus began to reveal his messianic identity in a very Jewish way. He did not shout aloud in the streets or cry out from the rooftops, "I am the Messiah." Instead, he took up the scroll of the prophet Isaiah and found the place that spoke of the coming of an "anointed" deliverer (see Isaiah 61:1–4). After reading Isaiah's prophecy, Jesus closed the scroll and said to his audience, "Today, this scripture has been fulfilled in your hearing" (Luke 4:21). With these words, he proclaimed to his fellow Jews that their long-held hope for the coming of the Messiah, the "anointed one" (Hebrew *mashiah*), had at last been fulfilled—in him. As we will see over the course of this book, this was the first of many instances in which Jesus would utilize the Jewish Scriptures to reveal himself to a Jewish audience as the long-awaited Jewish Messiah.

You Shall Not Drink the Blood

However, if Jesus did in fact see himself as the Jewish Messiah, then we are faced with a historical puzzle—a mystery of sorts. On the one hand, Jesus drew directly on the Jewish Scriptures as the inspiration for many of his most famous teachings. (Think once again of his sermon in the synagogue at Nazareth.) On the other hand, he said things that appeared to go directly against the Jewish Scriptures. Perhaps the most shocking of these are his teachings about eating his flesh and drinking his blood. According to the Gospel of John, in another Jewish synagogue on another Sabbath day, Jesus said the following words:

> "Amen, amen, I say to you, *unless you eat the flesh of the Son of Man and drink his blood*, you have no life in you; he who eats my flesh and drinks my blood has eternal life, and I will raise him up at the last day. For my flesh is food indeed, and my blood is drink indeed . . ." This he said in the synagogue, as he taught at Capernaum. (JOHN 6:53–54, 59)

And then again, at the Last Supper, on the night he was betrayed:

> Now, as they were eating, Jesus took bread, and
> blessed, and broke it, and gave it to the disciples
> and said, *"Take, eat; this is my body."* And he took a
> cup, and when he had given thanks he gave it to
> them, saying, *"Drink of it, all of you; for this is my blood
> of the covenant,* which is poured out for many for
> the forgiveness of sins." (MATTHEW 26:26–28)

What is the meaning of these strange words? What did
Jesus mean when he told his Jewish listeners in the synagogue that they had to eat his flesh and drink his blood in
order to have eternal life? And what did he mean when he
told his Jewish disciples that the bread of the Last Supper
was his "body" and the wine was his "blood"? Why did he
command them to eat and drink it?

We'll explore these questions and many others
throughout this book. For now, I simply want to point out
that the history of Christianity reveals dozens of different responses. Over the centuries, most Christians have
taken Jesus at his word, believing that the bread and wine
of the Eucharist really do become the body and blood of
Christ. Others, however, especially since the time of the
Protestant Reformation in the 1500s, think that Jesus was
speaking only symbolically. Still others, such as certain
modern historians, deny that Jesus could have said such
things, even though they are recorded in all four Gospels
and in the writings of Saint Paul (see Matthew 26:26–29;
Mark 14:22–25; Luke 22:14–30; John 6:53–58; 1 Corinthians 11:23–26).

The reasons for disagreement are several. First of all is
the shocking nature of Jesus' words. How could anyone,
even the Messiah, command his followers to eat his flesh
and drink his blood? As the Gospel of John records, when

Jesus' disciples first heard his teaching, they said, "This is a hard saying, who can listen to it?" (John 6:60). Jesus' words were so offensive to their ears that they could barely listen to him. And indeed, many of them left him, and "no longer walked with him" (John 6:66). And he let them go. From the very beginning, people found Jesus' command to eat his body and drink his blood extremely offensive.

Another reason for disagreement is somewhat more subtle. Even if Jesus *was* speaking literally about eating his flesh and drinking his blood, what could such a command even mean? Was he talking about cannibalism—eating the flesh of a human corpse? While there is no explicit commandment against cannibalism in the Jewish Bible, it was certainly considered taboo. Again, the Gospels bear witness to this reaction. "The Jews then disputed among themselves, saying, 'How can this man give us his flesh to eat?'" (John 6:52). This is a good question, and it deserves a good answer.

Perhaps the strongest objection to Jesus' words comes from Jewish Scripture itself. As any ancient Jew would have known, the Bible absolutely forbids a Jewish person to *drink the blood* of an animal. Although many Gentile religions considered drinking blood to be a perfectly acceptable part of pagan worship, the Law of Moses specifically prohibited it. God had made this very clear on several different occasions. Take, for example, the following Scriptures:

> Every moving thing that lives shall be food for you. . . . Only *you shall not eat flesh with its life, that is, its blood.* (GENESIS 9:3–4)

> If any man of the house of Israel or of the strangers that sojourns among them eats any blood, I will set my face against that person who eats blood, and

will cut him off from among his people. For *the life of the flesh is in the blood*; and I have given it for you upon the altar to make atonement for your souls; for it is the blood that makes atonement, by reason of its life. Therefore I have said to the people of Israel, No person among you shall eat blood, neither shall any stranger who sojourns among you eat blood. (LEVITICUS 17:10–12)

You may slaughter and eat flesh within any of your towns, as much as you desire. . . . *Only you shall not eat the blood*; you shall pour it out upon the earth like water. (DEUTERONOMY 12:16)

Clearly, the commandment against drinking animal blood was serious. To break it would mean being "cut off" from God and from his people. Notice also that it was a universal law. God expected not only the chosen people of Israel to keep it, but any Gentile "strangers" living among them. Finally, note the reason for the prohibition. People were not to consume blood because "the life" or "the soul" (Hebrew *nephesh*) of the animal is in the blood. As Leviticus states, "It is the blood that makes atonement, by *the power of its life*." While scholars continue to debate exactly what this means, one thing is clear: in the ancient world, the Jewish people were known for their refusal to consume blood. Jesus' words at the Last Supper become even more mysterious with this biblical background in mind. As a Jew, how could he ever have commanded his disciples to eat his flesh and drink his blood? Wouldn't this mean explicitly breaking the biblical law against consuming blood? Indeed, even if Jesus meant his words only *symbolically*, how could he say such things? Wouldn't his command mean transgressing the spirit of the Law, if not the letter? As the Jewish scholar Geza Vermes points out,

> [T]he imagery of eating a man's body and especially drinking his blood . . . , even after allowance is made for metaphorical language, strikes a totally foreign note in a Palestinian Jewish cultural setting (cf. John 6.52). With their profoundly rooted blood taboo, Jesus' listeners would have been overcome with nausea at hearing such words.

So, what should we make of these words of Jesus?

THROUGH ANCIENT JEWISH EYES

In this book, I will try to show that Jesus should be taken at his word. Along with the majority of Christians throughout history, I believe that Jesus himself taught that he was really and truly present in the Eucharist. In doing so, I will follow the Apostle Paul, a first-century Pharisee and an expert in the Jewish Law, when he said,

> I speak as to sensible men, judge for yourselves what I say. The cup of blessing which we bless, is it not a communion in the blood of Christ? The bread which we break, is it not a communion in the body of Christ? (1 CORINTHIANS 10:16)

My goal is to explain how a first-century Jew like Jesus, Paul, or any of the apostles, could go from believing that drinking *any* blood—much less human blood—was an abomination before God, to believing that drinking the blood of Jesus was actually *necessary* for Christians: "Unless you eat the flesh of the Son of Man and drink his blood, you have no life in you" (John 6:53).

In order to achieve this goal, we will have to go back in time to the first century A.D., in order to understand what Jesus was doing and saying in his original context. To a certain extent, this will mean taking off our modern "eyeglasses" and trying to see things as the first Jewish Christians saw them. When we look at the mystery of the Last Supper through ancient Jewish eyes, in the light of Jewish worship, beliefs, and hopes for the future, we will discover something remarkable. We will discover that there is much more in common between ancient Judaism and early Christianity than we might at first have expected. In fact, we will find that it was precisely the Jewish faith of the first Christians that enabled them to believe that the bread and wine of the Eucharist were really the body and blood of Jesus Christ.

Unfortunately, as soon as we try to do this, we are faced with a problem. In order for us to hear Jesus in the way his first disciples would have heard him, we need to be familiar with two key sources of information: (1) the Jewish *Scriptures*, commonly known as the Old Testament, and (2) ancient Jewish *tradition*, enshrined in writings not contained in the Jewish Bible.

Now, if my experience with students is any indicator, many modern readers—especially Christians—find the Jewish Scriptures to be challenging and unfamiliar territory. This is especially true of those passages in the Old Testament that describe ancient Jewish rituals, sacrifice, and worship—passages that will be very important for us as we explore Jesus' last meal with his friends before his crucifixion. As for ancient Jewish writings *outside* the Bible—such as the Mishnah and the Talmud—although many people have heard of them, they are often not widely read by non-Jewish readers aside from specialists in biblical studies.

For this reason, before beginning, it will be helpful to briefly identify the Jewish writings that I will be drawing on over the course of this book. (The reader may want to mark this page for future reference as we move along.) I want to stress here that I am not suggesting that Jesus himself would have read any of these, some of which were written down long after his death. What I am arguing is that many of them bear witness to ancient Jewish traditions that may have circulated at the time of Jesus and which demonstrate remarkable power to explain passages in the New Testament that reflect Jewish practices and beliefs.

With that in mind, after the Old Testament itself, some of the most important Jewish sources I will draw on are as follows:

- *The Dead Sea Scrolls*: an ancient collection of Jewish manuscripts copied sometime between the second century B.C. and A.D. 70. This collection contains numerous writings from the Second Temple period, during which Jesus lived.

- *The Works of Josephus*: a Jewish historian and Pharisee who lived in the first century A.D. Josephus' works are extremely important witnesses to Jewish history and culture at the time of Jesus and the early Church.

- *The Mishnah*: an extensive collection of the oral traditions of Jewish rabbis who lived from about 50 B.C.

to A.D. 200. Most of these traditions are focused on legal and liturgical matters. For rabbinic Judaism, the Mishnah remains the most authoritative witness to Jewish tradition outside of the Bible itself.

- *The Targums*: ancient Jewish translations and paraphrases of the Bible from Hebrew into Aramaic. These emerged sometime after the Babylonian exile (587 B.C.), when many Jews began speaking Aramaic rather than Hebrew. Scholars disagree about their exact dates.

- *The Babylonian Talmud*: a vast compilation—more than thirty volumes—of the traditions of Jewish rabbis who lived from around A.D. 220 to 500. The Talmud consists of both legal opinions and biblical interpretations, in the form of a massive commentary on the Mishnah.

- *The Midrashim*: ancient Jewish commentaries on various books of the Bible. Although parts of these are later than the Talmud, they contain many interpretations of Scripture attributed to rabbis who lived during the times of the Mishnah and the Talmud.

These are by no means all of the ancient Jewish writings that are relevant for understanding the New Testament, but they are the ones I will be looking at most frequently in this book.

In particular, I want to highlight the importance of the rabbinic literature: the Mishnah, the Talmud, and the Midrashim. Although many of these writings were edited after the time of Jesus himself, both rabbinic experts and

New Testament scholars agree that, if used with caution, they are still very important for us to study. For one thing, the rabbis often claim to be preserving traditions that go back to a time when the Temple still existed (before A.D. 70). In many cases, there are good reasons to take seriously these claims. Moreover, unlike the Dead Sea Scrolls or the writings of Josephus, the rabbinic literature continues to play an important role in the life of Jewish communities to this day. For this reason, I will pay particular attention to the Mishnah and the Talmud, which are still considered by many Jews to be the most authoritative witnesses to ancient Jewish tradition.

With all of this background in mind, we can now focus our attention on those ancient Jewish beliefs about the coming of the Messiah that may shed light on the Eucharistic words of Jesus. Unfortunately, many modern readers are only vaguely familiar with Jewish beliefs regarding the coming of the Messiah. In fact, a good deal of what most Christian readers have learned about Jewish messianic ideas is often oversimplified, riddled with exaggerations, or even downright false.

Therefore, in order for us to situate Jesus' teachings in their historical context, we need to back up a bit and answer a few broader questions: What were first-century Jews actually waiting for God to do? We know that many were expecting him to send the Messiah, but what did they think the Messiah would be like? What did they believe would happen when he finally came?

———————— ❧ ❧ ————————

2

WHAT WERE THE JEWISH PEOPLE WAITING FOR?

WHAT KIND OF MESSIAH?

If you ask most people today what the Jewish people were waiting for at the time of Jesus, you will probably hear something like this: "In the first century A.D., the Jewish people were waiting for an *earthly, political Messiah* to come and set them free from the Roman Empire and return the land of Israel to its rightful owners."

The notion of a purely political Messiah with purely political aims has become remarkably widespread, even among people who are not very familiar with either the Bible or ancient Judaism. I know this from personal experience, having spent the last several years traveling around the country and lecturing on Jesus and Judaism. In that time, I've repeatedly found that although many Christians admit to knowing very little about ancient Jewish practice and belief, the one thing they all seem to have heard is the idea that the Jewish people were waiting for only a military Messiah—a warrior king who would bring victory by defeating the empire of Caesar and reestablishing the earthly dominion of Israel.

And this is partially true. Some Jews at the time of Jesus were in fact only waiting for political deliverance from their Roman overlords. Chief among these were the Zealots, a first-century Jewish sect who were so called because of their zealous love for the land of Israel and their equally zealous hatred for Rome. However, to say that *all* Jews at the time of Jesus were simply waiting for a political Messiah is an exaggeration. While possessing a grain of truth, this thought does not do justice to the rich diversity of Jewish hopes for the future at the time of Jesus.

For if you actually pick up and read ancient Jewish writings themselves—especially the books of Jewish Scripture (the Old Testament) and the witnesses to ancient Jewish tradition (the Mishnah, the Targums, the Talmud)—you will find something quite surprising. You will find that many ancient Jews were waiting for much more than just a military Messiah. You will find that many of them were waiting for the restoration of Israel in a new exodus.

THE JEWISH HOPE FOR A NEW EXODUS

What was the Jewish hope for a new exodus? It was the expectation that the God of Israel would one day save his people in much the same way that he had saved them centuries before, at the time of Moses, the time of the first exodus. It was the hope that when the age of salvation finally dawned, God would recapitulate (or "recap") the events that had transpired during the flight from Egypt.

In order to understand this more clearly, we need to know the basics of the first exodus from Egypt. The story can be found in the Old Testament books of Exodus, Leviticus, Numbers, and Deuteronomy. It is here that we read the story of Moses, the deliverance of the twelve tribes of Jacob from slavery in Egypt, the plagues and the Passover, the wilderness wandering, and, ultimately, of the Israelites' journey home to the promised land of Canaan. It's the story of events that took place sometime in the late second millennium B.C., well over a thousand years before the birth of Jesus.

According to Jewish Scripture, this exodus from Egypt came to an end when Joshua finally led the twelve tribes into the promised land. Nevertheless, for reasons we will explore below, the Old Testament prophets also foretold that God would one day bring about a new exodus. The essentials of this new exodus can be summarized by four key events: (1) the coming of a new Moses; (2) the making of a new covenant; (3) the building of a new Temple; and (4) the journey to a new promised land.

As we will see, a proper understanding of the new exodus will not only shed light on what most Jews were waiting for at the time of Jesus. It will also help explain how Jesus deliberately sought to fulfill those hopes in himself, as the Jewish Messiah. In particular, the new exodus will provide us our three primary keys for unlocking the mystery of the Last Supper: the Passover, the Manna, and the Bread of the Presence.

Let's take a moment, then, to look at the basic components of this ancient Jewish hope for the future.

1. The New Moses

In the first exodus from Egypt, God had saved the people of Israel by means of a deliverer: Moses. According to the Old Testament prophets, God would one day save his people again by means of a new deliverer: the Messiah. From this perspective, the future deliverer would be like a new Moses.

With regard to the first Moses, his story is well known. At the time of Moses' birth, the twelve tribes of Israel—who were supposed to have inherited the land promised by God to Abraham—were in exile in the land of Egypt (see Genesis 15). Instead of reigning as a "kingdom of priests" in the promised land of Canaan, they languished in slavery under Pharaoh, the king of Egypt (Exodus 1–2). When Moses, who was himself an Israelite, had grown up, he was commissioned by God to deliver the tribes of Israel from the hand of the Egyptians and bring them home to the promised land, "a land flowing with milk and honey" (Exodus 3:7–12). According to the Bible, Moses did this by means of ten miraculous plagues, which climaxed in the death of every Egyptian firstborn son, the sacrifice of the Passover lamb, and the great crossing of the Red Sea (Exodus 7–15).

After bringing the Israelites out of Egypt, Moses spent forty years with them in the desert, patiently (and sometimes not so patiently) leading them to the promised land. At the very end of his life, on the very edge of the land of Canaan, he died, having carried out his divinely ordained mission. As the Bible says, when Moses died, there was "none like him" in all Israel; nor afterward did there arise in Israel any prophet "like Moses, whom the LORD knew face to face" (Deuteronomy 34:10–11).

This is where the story of Moses ends. But it is not the end of Israel's story, for in the millennium that transpired between the exodus from Egypt and the birth of Jesus, two major disasters struck the people of God, disasters that would give rise to the hope for a future act of deliverance by God. First, in 722 B.C., the ten northern tribes of Israel were taken into exile by the Assyrian empire and scattered among the surrounding Gentile nations (see 2 Kings 15–17). Over a century later, in 587 B.C., the two remaining southern tribes of Judah and Benjamin were likewise taken into exile, this time by the Babylonian empire (see 2 Kings 25–27). Although at this point God's promise of the land to the twelve tribes would appear to have been broken, alongside these tragic events there arose a hope that God would one day send his people a new deliverer, a new Moses.

In ancient Jewish tradition, this hope for a new Moses was actually rooted in the promise of Moses himself. According to the Book of Deuteronomy, shortly before Moses' death, he had prophesied that the twelve tribes of Israel would rebel against the Law of God and, as a result, be cast out of the promised land (Deuteronomy 4:26–27). In addition to these prophecies of future punishment, however, Moses also declares that God would one day send Israel another deliverer, a prophet like himself:

> [Moses said to the Israelites:] "The LORD your God will raise up for you *a prophet like me* from among you, from your brethren—him you shall heed. . . . And the LORD said to me, 'They have

rightly said all that they have spoken. I will raise up for them *a prophet like you* from among their brethren; and I will put my words in his mouth, and he shall speak all that I command him." (DEUTERONOMY 18:15–18)

In later Jewish tradition, these words were interpreted as a prophecy of the Messiah, the anointed one (*mashiah*) who would be a new Moses. Like Moses before him, the Messiah would one day be sent to Israel, in a time of great need, in order to deliver them from bondage. Take, for example, the words of Rabbi Berekiah, who lived in the third or fourth century A.D.:

> Rabbi Berekiah said in the name of Rabbi Isaac: "*As the first redeemer* [Moses] *was, so shall the latter Redeemer* [the Messiah] *be.* What is stated of the former redeemer? 'And Moses took his wife and his sons, and set them upon an ass' (Exod. 4:20). Similarly will it be with the latter Redeemer, as it is stated, 'Lowly and riding upon an ass' (Zech. 9:9). As the former redeemer caused manna to descend, as it is stated, 'Behold, I will cause to rain bread from heaven for you (Exod. 16:4)', so will the latter Redeemer cause manna to descend, as it is stated, 'May he be as a rich grainfield in the land' (Ps. 72:16). (*ECCLESIASTES RABBAH* 1:28)

As anyone familiar with the Gospel accounts of Jesus' triumphal entry into Jerusalem can see, the tradition of the Messiah coming on a donkey was alive and well in the first century (Matthew 21:1–11; Mark 11:1–10; Luke 19:29–38; John 12:12–18). For our purposes here, the main point is that in this particular rabbinic tradition, the Messiah is clearly expected to be a new Moses, whose actions would parallel the actions of the first Moses. Just as Moses had gone out of Egypt using a donkey, so, too, the rabbis said the Messiah would come, humble and "riding upon a donkey," thereby fulfilling the biblical prophecy of Zechariah. And just as Moses had caused the miraculous manna to descend from above, so, too, the rabbis said that the Messiah would one day rain down bread from heaven.

2. The New Covenant

In the first exodus, God had made a covenant—a sacred family bond—between himself and the people of Israel. This covenant was sealed with the blood of sacrifice and concluded by a heavenly banquet. In the new exodus, so the Old Testament prophets foretold, God would make a new covenant with his people, one that would never be broken.

A good case can be made that the making of the first covenant is one of the most important moments in the exodus from Egypt. This event took place when the twelve tribes of Israel arrived at the foot of Mount Sinai. It was there that they entered into a new relationship with God and began receiving divine instructions for how they would worship him. Indeed, according to Scripture, the primary reason for the exodus from Egypt was precisely so that Israel might freely worship God. As God commanded Moses to tell Pharaoah, "Israel is my first-born son. . . . Let my son go that he may *worship* me" (Exodus 4:22–23). Contrary to popular opinion, the exodus was not some kind of divine real-estate grab; nor was it simply about delivering the people from political slavery. In the end, it was about worship. In the end, it was about establishing a sacred family relationship between God and the people by means of a covenant.

That is why Moses and the Israelites are so intent on beginning to offer sacrifice to God as soon as they arrive at Mount Sinai. According to the Bible, shortly after receiving the Ten Commandments (Exodus 19–20), Moses "built an altar at the foot of the mountain, and twelve pillars, according to the twelve tribes of Israel" (Exodus 24:4). And by means of sacrificial worship, Moses and the Israelites sealed their covenant relationship with God:

> And [Moses] sent young men of the sons of Israel, who offered burnt offerings and sacrificed peace offerings of oxen to the LORD. And Moses took half of the blood and put it in basins, and half of the blood he threw against the altar. Then he took *the book of the covenant,* and read it in the hearing of the people. . . . And Moses took *the blood of the covenant* and threw it upon the people, and said, "*Behold, the blood of the covenant* which the LORD has made with you in accordance with all these words." Then Moses and Aaron, Nadab and Abihu, and seventy of the elders of Israel went up, and they saw the God of Israel; and there was under his feet as it were a pavement of sapphire stone, like the very heaven for clearness. And he did not lay his hand on the chief men of the people of Israel; *they beheld God, and ate and drank.* (EXODUS 24:5–11)

Two things stand out here. First, notice that the exodus covenant is sealed in blood. This is symbolized and realized by Moses' act of throwing "the blood of the covenant" upon the altar—which represents God—and the people, who represent Israel. By means of this ritual, God makes Israel to be his own family, his own "flesh and blood." By means of this action, they now share the same blood; they are now family. Second, notice also that the making of the covenant does not end with the death of the sacrificial animals, but with a banquet—a heavenly meal.

From the perspective of the covenant, this makes sense. One of the main things families do is eat together. But this meal on Mount Sinai was no ordinary feast. In fact, in the history of Israel, nothing like this would ever happen again. Once the blood of the covenant is poured out upon the altar, Moses and the elders not only go up the mountain, they are taken up into "heaven" itself, where they feast in the presence of God. "They beheld God, and ate and drank" (Exodus 24:11).

Unfortunately, as the Old Testament makes clear, the joy of this heavenly banquet did not last long. Shortly thereafter, at the foot of Mount Sinai, many of the Israelites broke the covenant with God by worshiping the golden calf (Exodus 32). And this was just the beginning. Year after year, generation after generation, countless Israelites abandoned the Mosaic covenant by going after other gods and entering into covenants with them instead.

But God did not give up on his people. Almost a thousand years after the time of Moses, the prophet Jeremiah would proclaim that God was going to make a new covenant, one that would be even greater than the covenant with Moses:

> Behold, the days are coming, says the LORD, when I will make *a new covenant* with the house of Israel and the house of Judah, *not like the covenant which I made with their fathers when I took them*

by the hand to bring them out of the land of Egypt, my
covenant which they broke, though I was their
husband, says the LORD. But this is the covenant
which I will make with the house of Israel after
those days, says the LORD: I will put my law within
them, and I will write it upon their hearts; and I
will be their God, and they shall be my people.
(JEREMIAH 31:31–33)

In these words, the connection between the exodus
covenant and the new covenant is very clear. For one
thing, this new covenant, like the covenant at Mount Sinai,
will be made with all twelve tribes of Israel. That is what
Jeremiah means when he speaks of "the house of Israel,"
referring to the ten northern tribes exiled in 722 B.C.,
and "the house of Judah," referring to the two southern
tribes exiled in 587 B.C. In other words, despite the tragic
exiles of the Israelites from the promised land, when God
makes the new covenant, he will make it with all twelve
tribes. Moreover, Jeremiah explicitly contrasts this new
covenant with the covenant at Mount Sinai. The new covenant will be greater than the covenant made when God
brought the Israelites "out of the land of Egypt." Although
Jeremiah himself does not say so, one can ask, Will the
new covenant, like the old, be sealed with sacrifice? And
will it, too, climax with a heavenly meal?

Curiously, rabbinic literature does not have much to
say about the new covenant, except to insist that it had not
yet taken place. For example, according to Rabbi Hezekiah, who probably lived in the third century A.D., Jeremiah's prophecy would only be fulfilled at the end of the
age, when "this World" will end and "the World to Come"
will begin.

However, this does not mean that the rabbis forgot about the covenant *banquet* of Mount Sinai. On the contrary, the heavenly meal described in Exodus 24 became a rabbinic image or prefiguration of the messianic age of salvation. According to Jewish tradition, in the new world created by God, the righteous will no longer feast on earthly food and drink, but on the "presence" of God:

> In the World to Come there is no eating or drinking . . . but the righteous sit with crowns on their heads *feasting on the brightness of the divine presence*, as it says, "And they beheld God, and did eat and drink (Exod 24:11)." (BABYLONIAN TALMUD, BERAKOTH 17A)

Obviously, this ancient vision of the future is about much more than a military Messiah! As the Jewish scholar Joseph Klausner once pointed out, this rabbinic tradition describes an age when "the vision of God" will take the place of earthly "eating and drinking." It is a hope for the covenant renewed, and for the heavenly banquet of God's people to be resumed, so that they might feast forever, not on earthly food and drink, but on "the divine presence" itself.

3. The New Temple

In the first exodus, the worship of God was centered on the Tabernacle of Moses, the portable "temple" that Israel used while traveling in the wilderness. In the new exodus, the prophets foretold, the worship of God would take place in a new Temple, which would be more glorious than either the Tabernacle of Moses or the Temple of Solomon had ever been.

In order to understand the Jewish hope for a new Temple, we need to remember that before the exodus from Egypt, during the time of the Patriarchs, there was no central place of worship. Almost two thousand years before the birth of Jesus, Abraham, Isaac, and Jacob all worshiped God wherever they were, building altars of stones and wood in various places throughout the promised land. However, *after* the twelve tribes of Israel left Egypt and made their covenant with God, the very first thing God did was command his people to build him one place of worship—the Tabernacle—in which the priests of Israel would worship God by means of sacrifice. In fact, almost half the Book of Exodus is devoted to describing the Tabernacle and how it was built, often in painful detail. (See Exodus 25–40, but be warned. This is where many readers of the Bible begin to doze off!)

In terms of size, the Tabernacle of Moses seems to have been a rather small building—about 75 feet wide and 150 feet long. Nevertheless, its physical size was no indicator of its spiritual importance. According to the Book of Exodus, it consisted of three parts. First, there was the so-called Outer Court, which contained the Bronze Altar of sacrifice on which the priests would offer animal sacrifices to God. Second, moving inward, there was the Holy Place, which contained three sacred objects: the golden Lampstand (in Hebrew, the *menorah*), the golden Altar of Incense, and the golden table of twelve cakes of bread, known as the Bread of the Presence (see Exodus 25). In this Holy Place, the priests of Israel would worship God through the unbloody offering of incense, bread, and wine. Third and finally, there was the Holy of Holies, the innermost sanctum that housed the golden Ark of the Covenant, which contained the tablets of the Ten Commandments, an urn of the manna, and the staff of Aaron (see Hebrews 9:1–5). Apart from being the place of worship, the reason the Tabernacle was so important to the ancient Israelites was that they saw it as the dwelling place of God on earth. That's why they called it the Tent of Meeting: there, God would "meet" with them, in the form of a cloud of "glory" descending from heaven (see Exodus 40:34–38).

For our purposes, the main point is that the Tabernacle of Moses, the place of worship during the exodus, became the prototype for a permanent place of worship in the promised land: the Temple of Solomon. This Temple, built several hundred years after Moses, and almost a thousand years before the birth of Jesus, was essentially a bigger and much more splendid version of the Tabernacle (1 Kings 6–8). It, too, was the dwelling place of God on earth, and the place of sacrificial worship. It, too, was divided into three parts, with the golden Menorah, the Altar of Incense, the Bread of the Presence, and the Ark of the Covenant at its center. However, unlike the Tabernacle, which was a portable tent, the Temple of Solomon was a building of stone, lavishly covered "with gold," and decorated with carvings of golden angels, palm trees, and open flowers (1 Kings 8:22–32). Given such descriptions, it should come as no surprise that the Temple in Jerusalem was the pride and joy of all Israel.

Tragically, however, Solomon's Temple did not last very long. Only a few centuries after it was completed, it was destroyed by the Babylonian empire. In 587 B.C., when the Babylonians invaded the promised land, they not only captured the southern tribes of Judah, they also burned the city of Jerusalem, razing the Temple to the ground (2 Kings 25). This was the time of the Babylonian exile, when the people of Judah were taken out of the promised land to live among the Gentiles. But this situation did not last forever. Eventually, Babylon gave way to the Persian empire, and King Cyrus of Persia was of a different mind toward the Jewish people. Around 539 B.C., Cyrus not only allowed the Jews to return to the land; he also gave them permission to rebuild the Temple (Ezra 1). Nevertheless, the new Temple—known as the Second Temple—was by no means as glorious as the Temple of Solomon. In fact, the Bible says that when the Second Temple was built, "the old men" who had seen the first Temple wept, because it did not compare to the glory of Solomon's Temple (Ezra 3:10–13).

Indeed, over the course of Israel's tragic history, the Old Testament prophets had spoken with greater and greater frequency of a future Temple, a *new Temple*, that God would eventually build in the age of salvation, at the time of the new exodus.

For example, the prophet Micah declares that in the latter days, God would establish "the mountain of the house of the LORD"—that is, the Temple mount—as the highest of the mountains of the earth (Micah 4:1–2). Anyone who has been to Jerusalem knows that the little hill on which Solomon's Temple was built is hardly the "highest" of all the mountains of the earth! This is a prophecy of a new Temple, the final Temple of the end-times. Along similar lines, Isaiah speaks of a coming day when God will glorify his Temple, so that it would become "a house of prayer for all peoples" (Isaiah 56:6–7; 60:1–7). The prophet Ezekiel says that when the new David (the Messiah) finally comes, God will set his "sanctuary" in the midst of Israel for evermore, and the Gentiles will convert to the worship of the LORD (Ezekiel 37:24–28). Finally, the prophet Haggai even goes so far as to claim that the splendor of the future Temple would be "greater than the former"—that is, greater even than Solomon's Temple (Haggai 2:6–9). Given the weeping of the Jewish elders at the building of the Second Temple, this prophecy can only refer to a future Temple—the new Temple of the last days.

In short, the Old Testament prophets bear constant witness to a shining hope for a new Temple, which would not only recapture the lost glory of Solomon's Temple but even exceed it.

The same holds true for Jewish texts outside the Bible. They, too, speak of the hope for a new Temple. For example, the Dead Sea Scrolls, which come from shortly before and during the lifetime of Jesus, contain multiple prophecies of a future Temple. In fact, one of the longest scrolls found, the *Temple Scroll*, consists of more than sixty columns of detailed descriptions of the new Temple. Likewise, the ancient Jewish rabbis believed there would one day be a new Temple. For one thing, they appear to have prayed for the restoration of Temple worship on a daily basis, begging God in daily prayer to "bring back the worship into the Holy of Holies of thy house" (*Shemoneh 'Esreh* 17). Intriguingly, some rabbis also believed that the new Temple would be built by the Messiah himself. As one rabbinic commentary teaches:

> *When the King Messiah who abides in the north will awaken he will come and build the Temple*, which is situated in the south. This accords with the text, "I have roused up one from the north, and he is come (Isa 41:25)," etc. (*NUMBERS RABBAH* 13:2)

This hope for a new Temple is extremely important for understanding ancient Jewish expectations of the future. During Jesus' own lifetime, King Herod and his successors had spent much of their time and money transforming the second Temple into one of the wonders of the ancient world (see John 2:20). But the second Temple also had many problems, not least of which was the fact that the Holy of Holies was *empty*, the Ark of the Covenant having been lost since the destruction of Jerusalem centuries before. As Josephus tells us, during the first century A.D., inside the Holy of Holies was "nothing at all" (*War* 5:219).

Given this situation, it should come as no surprise that many Jews were still waiting for the glorious new Temple that the prophets had said would be built at the time of the coming of the Messiah.

4. The New Promised Land

In the first exodus from Egypt, the twelve tribes of Israel set out on a journey to the promised land, the land of Canaan, which God had promised to give to Abraham and his children. In the new exodus, the prophets foretold, God would bring both Israel and the Gentile nations into a new promised land, and they would possess this land forever (Isaiah 60:21).

With regard to the first exodus, the story of the land is well known. It begins when God calls Abraham from his home in Ur of the Chaldeans (present-day Iraq) and promises to give him and his descendants "the land" of Canaan (present-day Israel) (Genesis 12:1–3). The promise appears to have been fulfilled at first. Isaac, the son of Abraham, and Jacob, Abraham's grandson, did indeed dwell in the land (Genesis 22–36). Nevertheless, through a series of events involving Joseph and the twelve sons of Jacob, the descendants of Abraham, Isaac, and Jacob eventually ended up living in Egypt, *outside* the promised land, for some four hundred years, until the time of Moses (Genesis 37–50). As we saw earlier, from the birth of Moses to the crossing of the Jordan River by Joshua, the story of the exodus from Egypt is essentially the story of the twelve tribes' return to the land promised to Abraham. It is the story of God's bringing his people out of slavery and exile and into a "broad land, a land flowing with milk and honey" (Exodus 3:8).

However, the story does not end there. For the people of Israel did not remain in the land forever. As I mentioned earlier, in 722 B.C., ten of the twelve tribes of Israel were cast out of the promised land by the Assyrian empire and scattered among the Gentile nations. A couple of centuries later, in 587 B.C., history repeated itself, and the Babylonian empire came and did the same to the remaining two tribes of Judah and Benjamin, taking them into Babylon. Now, although in 539 B.C. the two southern tribes had returned to the land of Israel, by the time we get to the first century—the time of Jesus—the ten northern tribes remained scattered and lost among the nations. (This is the origin of the legend of the "lost tribes of Israel.") For this reason, and because of God's sworn promise to give the land to Abraham, the Old Testament prophets foretold that one day, there would be a final "return to the land," a new exodus to a new promised land.

This hope for a new exodus, for the ingathering of God's scattered people, can be found all over the pages of Jewish Scripture. For example, the prophet Amos declares that one day God will plant his people "upon their land," so that they shall never be "plucked up out of the land which I have given them" (Amos 9:14–15). Likewise, Hosea foretells that at the time of the new covenant, all twelve tribes will be sown once again in "the land" (Hosea 1:10–11; 2:16–23). Finally, Jeremiah declares that when the new exodus takes place, God will give the twelve tribes "a pleasant land" as their heritage (Jeremiah 3:15–19). And there are many other such prophecies.

What is fascinating about this biblical hope, however, is that there are hints that the *future* promised land would not necessarily be identical to the earthly land of Israel. This is already implicit in Nathan's famous prophecy of the everlasting kingdom of David (2 Samuel 7). In this oracle, God promises to "appoint *a place* for my people Israel" and to "plant them that they may dwell in their own place" (2 Samuel 7:10). But this new "place" cannot refer to the land of Israel, since at the time of David, all twelve tribes were *already* living in the land. Equally intriguing, the prophet Ezekiel describes the future promised land as being "like the garden of Eden" (Ezekiel 36:33–35) and ties the return of the twelve tribes of Israel to the resurrection of the dead (Ezekiel 37). Is this merely a reference to the land of Canaan? Or does Ezekiel envision a journey to some greater place?

Finally, and most important of all, the Book of Isaiah repeatedly describes the new exodus in terms of God's people journeying to a new Jerusalem (see Isaiah 43, 49, 60). Remarkably, Isaiah's vision portrays both the future Jerusalem and the future land as part of a "new heavens and a new earth"—that is, an entirely new creation:

> For behold, I create *new heavens and a new earth*;
> and the former things shall not be remembered
> or come into mind.

> But be glad and rejoice in that which I create;
> For behold, *I create Jerusalem* a rejoicing and
>   her people a joy . . .
>
>   (ISAIAH 64:17–18)

> For I know their works and their thoughts, and I
> am coming to gather all nations and tongues. . . .
> *And they shall bring all your brethren from all the nations*
> *as an offering to the LORD . . . to my holy mountain*
> *Jerusalem,* says the LORD. . . . For as *the new heavens*
> *and the new earth* which I will make shall remain
> before me, says the LORD; so shall your descen-
> dants remain. (ISAIAH 65:18, 20, 22)

In other words, within the Jewish Scriptures themselves, there are reasons to believe that the prophets envi-
sioned a new exodus to a new promised land, one that
would be greater than the promised land of the exodus
from Egypt.

When we turn to Jewish writings outside the Bible, we
continue to find evidence for a hope that is greater than
a merely earthly return to the land. For example, in one
ancient Jewish writing from the first century A.D., we discover the idea that the true "holy land" is in the "upper
world," where God's throne dwells. Unlike the earthly
land of Canaan, the heavenly promised land will exist forever, and is even identified as the "kingdom" of God (see
Testament of Job 33:1–9). Even more important is the witness of the Mishnah, which has this to say:

> *All Israelites have a share in the world to come,* for it is
> written, "Your people also shall all be righteous,
> *they shall inherit the land for ever,* the branch of my

planting, the work of my hands that I may be glo-
rified (Isa 60:21)." (MISHNAH, *SANHEDRIN* 10:1)

As scholars have recognized, in this Jewish tradition,
"inheriting the land" is equated with having a share in "the
world to come"—a common rabbinic expression for the
new world of the age of salvation. This interpretation of
the Mishnah is confirmed by the later Babylonian Talmud.
According to the Talmud, the return of the lost tribes of
Israel to the promised land is explicitly identified as their
entry into "the future world" (*Sanhedrin* 110b). This equa-
tion of the promised land with the future world is significant, for it shows that even rabbinic Judaism—which is
often characterized as very "this-worldly" in its hopes for
the future—could see the earthly promised land as a sign
of a *future* creation. And it is no coincidence that both the
Mishnah and the Talmud cite the vision of the new Jerusalem in Isaiah 60:21 as the basis for this future hope.

In short, for at least some ancient Jews, especially those
influenced by the Book of Isaiah, although the first exodus
had involved a return to the earthly promised land, the
new exodus would be different. It would involve a journey
to a new promised land, and a new Jerusalem. Apparently,
this new land would be far greater than that which had
been promised to Moses. It would be no ordinary land,
but a part of "the World to Come."

By now it should be clear that while *some* Jews may have
been waiting for a merely military Messiah, this was not
necessarily the case for all. According to the Jewish Scriptures and certain ancient Jewish traditions, for others, the
hope for the future consisted of much, much more. It was
a hope for the coming of the Messiah, who would not just
be a king, but a prophet and a miracle worker like Moses.

It was a hope for the making of a new and everlasting covenant, which would climax in a heavenly banquet where the righteous would see God, and feast on the divine presence. It was the hope for the building of a glorious new Temple, where God would be worshiped forever and ever. Finally, it was a hope for the ingathering of God's people into the promised land of a world made new. As the Lord had said in the Book of Isaiah:

> Remember not the former things, nor consider
>   the things of old.
> Behold, *I am doing a new thing*; now it springs
>   forth, do you not perceive it?
> I will make a way in the wilderness and rivers
>   in the desert.
>   (ISAIAH 43:18–19)

In short, according to the Old Testament and ancient Jewish tradition, the hope of God's people was for the restoration of Israel from exile, the ingathering of the Gentile nations, and the renewal of creation itself. It was a hope that God, by means of a new exodus, would one day "make all things new" (Revelation 21:5).

JESUS AND THE NEW EXODUS

With all this in mind, we can now ask the key question: Is there any reason to believe that Jesus *himself* was waiting for a new exodus?

As one might expect, given what I've said so far, the answer is "Yes," and that the hope for a new exodus helps a great deal in sorting out the meanings of Jesus' words and actions. However, before we dive into the details that will be pertinent for understanding the Last Supper specifically, it will be helpful to show Jesus' expectation of the new exodus in a more general way, by making a few brief points.

First, it is important to note that at the time of Jesus, the Jewish hope for a new exodus was not just something buried in the ancient oracles of the Hebrew prophets. To the contrary, the Jewish historian Josephus gives us reports suggesting that the idea of a new exodus was so widespread in the first century A.D. that several popular Jewish figures actually promised to be able to perform miracles that would hearken back to the exodus from Egypt. As an example, consider the following two accounts:

> During the period when Fadus was proconsul of Judaea, a certain imposter named Theudas persuaded the majority of the masses to take up their possessions and to follow him to the Jordan River. He stated that he was a prophet and that at his command the river would be parted and would provide them an easy passage.
>
> (JOSEPHUS, *ANTIQUITIES* 20:97–98)

> At this time there came to Jerusalem a man from Egypt who declared that he was a prophet and advised the masses of the common people to go out with him to the mountain called the Mount of Olives, which lies opposite the city. . . . For he asserted that he wished to demonstrate from there that at his command Jerusalem's walls

would fall down, through which he promised to provide them an entrance to the city.

(JOSEPHUS, *ANTIQUITIES* 20:169–170)

These figures, which modern scholars refer to as "sign prophets," were clearly modeling themselves on the two most memorable leaders of the exodus: Moses, who parted the waters of the Red Sea (Exodus 15), and Joshua, who miraculously brought down the walls of the city of Jericho (Joshua 6). Indeed, both Theudas and the Egyptian were popular enough to merit being mentioned not only by Josephus, but by Rabbi Gamaliel in the Acts of the Apostles (see Acts 5:33–39). Unfortunately for both of them, nothing ever came of their promises of miracles; Theudas was captured by the Roman procurator and beheaded, while the imperial cavalry slaughtered four hundred of the Egyptian's followers, he himself barely escaping alive. For our purposes, the main point is that the existence of such figures demonstrates that at the time of Jesus, the Jewish hopes for a new Moses and a new exodus were alive and well among the "common people."

With this historical context in mind, when we turn to the Gospels, it seems clear that many of Jesus' words and deeds also function as signs of the long-awaited new exodus. Like Theudas and the Egyptian, Jesus said and did things in public that would have evoked the memories of the exodus from Egypt. But unlike Theudas and the Egyptian, Jesus not only promised miraculous signs of the new exodus; he actually performed them.

For example, as we saw above, the Jewish Scripture foretells the coming of a future prophet like Moses (Deuteronomy 18). So how does Jesus begin his public ministry? By going out into the desert and fasting for "forty days," just as Moses had fasted for "forty days and forty nights" in the desert, atop Mount Sinai (Exodus 34:28). Moreover, in the Gospel of John, Jesus transforms water into wine as "the first of his signs" (John 2:1–11), just as Moses had transformed water into blood as one of the first "signs" against Pharaoh, in the exodus from Egypt (Exodus 7:14–24). By means of such actions, Jesus is in effect saying to his Jewish audience: "I am the new Moses, come to inaugurate the new exodus."

Likewise, according to the prophet Jeremiah, at the time of the new exodus, God will make a "new covenant" with his people, which will be greater than "the covenant" made when God brought them "out of the land of Egypt" (Jeremiah 31:31–32). So, how does Jesus end his public ministry? In the Upper Room, on the night before he died, he takes a cup of wine and says, "This cup which is poured out for you is the new covenant in my blood" (Luke 22:20; 1 Corinthians 11:25). By means of this act, Jesus is likewise saying; "I am fulfilling the prophecy of the new covenant through my own death."

Perhaps most striking of all, when Jesus is asked point blank by the disciples of John the Baptist whether he is in fact the Messiah, he replies by alluding to one of Isaiah's prophecies of the new exodus:

> "Go and tell John what you hear and see: the blind receive their sight and the lame walk, lepers are cleansed and the deaf hear, and the dead are raised up, and the poor have good news preached to them. And blessed is he who takes no offense at me."
>
> (MATTHEW 11:4–5; LUKE 4:18–19)

> Then the eyes of the blind shall be opened,
> and the ears of the deaf unstopped;
> then shall the lame man leap like a hart,
> and the tongue of the dumb sing for joy.
> For waters shall break forth in the wilderness,
> and streams in the desert . . .
> And a highway shall be there, and it shall be called
>   the Holy Way . . .
> And the ransomed of the LORD shall return,
>   and come to Zion [= Jerusalem] with singing . . .
>
> (ISAIAH 35:5–10)

In effect, Jesus is saying to the disciples of John, "My miracles are the signs of the new exodus spoken of by Isaiah, and I am the messianic herald of salvation."

In short, when viewed through ancient Jewish eyes, in the light of their common hopes for the future, Jesus' public ministry was literally brimming with signs of the long-awaited new exodus. He seems quite clearly to have been deliberately modeling his actions both on the Jewish Scripture and Jewish traditions about the coming of the Messiah.

Before closing this chapter, it is worth noting that the connection between Jesus and the exodus was not lost on the Gospel writers. In particular, Luke brings out the importance of this hope in his account of Jesus' transfiguration. There we find these remarkable words:

> [Jesus] took with him Peter and John and James, and went up on the mountain to pray. And as he was praying, the appearance of his countenance was altered and his clothing became dazzling white. And behold, two men talked with him, Moses and Elijah, who appeared in glory and

spoke of *his exodus, which he was to accomplish at Jerusalem.* (LUKE 9:28–31)

Although some versions of the Bible say that Jesus spoke of his "departure," the actual Greek word here is *exodos,* "exodus." Both translations are essentially correct; *exodos* means "a going out" or "departure," and was used to refer to the exodus from Egypt and as a euphemism for death. But, in a first-century Jewish context, Luke's selection of this particular word is pregnant with meaning. For it provides us with an essential clue as to *when* the new exodus would actually be fulfilled: during Jesus' passion and death in Jerusalem.

Indeed, the entire account of Jesus' transfiguration suggests that this new exodus, although based on the old, would be both similar and radically different. In the old exodus, God had identified Israel as his son: "Israel is my first-born son, and I say to you, 'Let my son go that he may worship me'" (Exodus 4:22). In the new exodus, spoken of during the Transfiguration, God says of Jesus: "This is my Son, my Chosen, listen to him" (Luke 9:35). In other words, Jesus is not *just* a new Moses. He is also the new Israel, the chosen Son of God, who will undergo the new exodus in his own person. By means of his passion and death—his "departure" in Jerusalem—Jesus himself will lead the people of God to the new promised land of the "new creation" (Matthew 19:28).

Of course, if these connections are correct, they raise more questions than answers. The first is this: If Jesus expected there to be a new exodus, how exactly did he think it would begin?

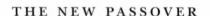

3

THE NEW PASSOVER

As we saw in the last chapter, many Jewish people living at the time of Jesus were not just waiting for an earthly Messiah to come and set them free from the grip of the Roman empire. Nor were they merely waiting for a political savior to establish a perfect society. Many of them were waiting for something much greater. They were waiting for a new exodus.

This ancient Jewish hope is important because it provides us with our first key to unlocking the mystery of the Last Supper. As any ancient Jew would have known, *if there is going to be a new exodus, then it would seem that there would need to be a new Passover as well.*

In the first exodus, the twelve tribes of Jacob did not just walk out of Egypt. They were delivered by God. At the time of Moses, the people of Israel did not simply decide one day to throw off the shackles of slavery. They were ransomed by the Lord. And while Moses performed a whole series of signs and plagues leading up to the exodus from Egypt, ultimately it was the Passover that set in motion the exodus of Israel. On that night, those Israelites who sacrificed the Passover lambs were not only saved from the angel of death, they were freed from slavery in Egypt. As a result, that night was revered as one of the most important events in the history of Israel. As the centuries passed, the Jewish people celebrated the memorial of the Passover of Egypt as the foremost of all feasts. Every year, millions of Jews—including Joseph, Mary, Jesus, and all of his disciples—would go up to Jerusalem to keep the Passover and celebrate the exodus from Egypt (Luke 2:41).

But at his final Passover, on the night of the Last Supper, Jesus did something strange. During that meal, instead of speaking about the past exodus from Egypt, Jesus talked about his future suffering and death. On that night, instead of explaining the meaning of the flesh of the Passover lamb, Jesus identified the bread and wine of the supper as his own body and blood, and commanded the disciples to eat and drink. Why?

The answer, I suggest, can be found in the Jewish hope for a new exodus. Although the Last Supper was a Passover meal, it was not ordinary. On that night, Jesus was not just celebrating one more memorial of the exodus from Egypt. Rather, he was establishing *a new Passover*, the long-awaited Passover of the Messiah. By means of *this* sacrifice, Jesus would inaugurate the new exodus, which the prophets had foretold and for which the Jewish people had been waiting. It is this connection between the Last Supper and the new Passover that will provide us with our first clue to answering the riddle of how Jesus could have commanded the disciples to eat his body and drink his blood.

However, if we are going to be able to see Jesus' actions through ancient Jewish eyes, we first need to study the meaning of the Passover itself, both in Jewish Scripture and in Jewish tradition. It will do us no good to begin talking about how Jesus instituted a new Passover if we are unfamiliar with the Passover of Egypt, as well as the meaning it held for Jews in the first century. Although the basic story is familiar to many, for our purposes, it is the details that matter. So before turning to the Last Supper itself, let's first go back to what the Passover was like in the Old Testament and at the time of Jesus.

THE BIBLICAL ROOTS OF PASSOVER

In order to understand Jesus' actions at the Last Supper in their ancient Jewish context, it is important first to study the shape of the Passover in Scripture itself. Although the Passover is mentioned numerous times in the pages of the Bible, the most important description is found in Exodus 12. This account not only tells the story of what happened on the night of the first Passover but also gives detailed instructions for how the people of Israel were supposed to keep the feast. From that night onward, all the way down to the time of Jesus (and beyond), the Passover would be celebrated each spring as a "day of remembrance," an ordinance that was to be carried out "forever" (Exodus 12:14). In other words, the Book of Exodus not only tells the history of what happened on Passover night. It also lays out the paschal *liturgy*—the sacrificial ritual—that was to be carried out by the Jewish people on that first night and for all time.

This biblical Passover liturgy is important because it will set the stage for later developments in Jewish tradition, as well as what Jesus will do at the Last Supper. Hence, it is important to pay attention to the various commands that God gave to Moses for the people to carry out. Although any ancient practicing Jew would have been familiar with God's instructions for keeping the first Passover, it will be helpful for us to refresh our memory and review the basic steps laid out in the Old Testament.

Step 1: Choose an Unblemished Male Lamb

The first step in the Passover sacrifice was for every man to choose an unblemished male lamb, a year old, to be offered as a sacrifice on behalf of his family. As God says to Moses regarding the Passover,

> This month shall be for you the beginning of months; it shall be the first month of the year for you. Tell all the congregation of Israel that on the tenth day of this month *they shall take every man a lamb* according to their father's houses, a lamb for a household. . . . Your lamb shall be without blemish, a male a year old; you shall take it from the sheep or from the goats; and you shall keep it until the fourteenth day of this month. (EXODUS 12:1–6)

It's important to note that the Passover lamb is explicitly required to be a male, in its prime (one year old) and "unblemished." This last characteristic meant that it could not be just any lamb. It had to be free of defects. The lamb could not be maimed or lame or diseased in any way. It had to be perfect.

Step 2: Sacrifice the Lamb

The second step was for the father of each household to sacrifice the lamb. The sacrifice took place on the fourteenth day of the month of Nisan, in the springtime, around March/April. As God says to Moses,

> You shall keep [the lamb] until the fourteenth day of this month, when the whole assembly of the congregation of Israel shall kill their lambs in the evening. (EXODUS 12:6)

During the sacrifice of the lamb, it was extremely important that not a single bone of the lamb be broken. "You shall not break a bone of it" (Exodus 12:46). In other words, the unblemished lamb was to be sacrificed whole, without marring its perfection in any way.

It's necessary to point out here that the sacrifice of the lamb was a specifically *priestly* action. Although modern readers sometimes forget the fact, in ancient Israel, no one but a priest could offer a blood sacrifice. That is what priests did; they were set apart for sacrificial worship. The reason this matters for us is that at the time of the exodus from Egypt, the priestly right of offering sacrifice belonged to all twelve tribes of Israel. All twelve tribes were called to be "a kingdom of priests" (Exodus 19:6). At the time of the exodus, there existed in Israel what might be called the "natural priesthood" of fathers and sons, so that "every man" (Exodus 12:3) would act as priest over his own household by both selecting and sacrificing the Passover lamb.

Later on, this privilege of offering sacrifice would be taken away from the eleven tribes and given to only one: the tribe of Levi. This happened when the majority of the tribes of Israel fell into idolatry and worshiped the Golden Calf (see Exodus 32). In the wake of this tragic event, the Levites were "ordained" to the priestly worship of the God of Israel, because they alone responded to Moses' call to renounce idolatry and come to the Lord's side (Exodus 32:39). From that point forward in the history of Israel, all the way down till Jesus' own day, only Levites were allowed to serve as priests in the Temple by offering blood sacrifice. If you were from the tribe of Reuben, or the tribe of Simeon, or even the royal tribe of Judah, you were prohibited from going up to the altar to pour out the blood of sacrifice.

But at the time of the *first* Passover, it was not so. At that time, before the worship of the Golden Calf, men from *all twelve tribes* of Israel acted as priests, offering the sacrifice of the Passover lamb in order to ransom their people and deliver them from death.

Step 3: Spread the Blood of the Lamb

The third step in the Passover sacrifice was to spread the blood of the lamb on the entryways of the homes of all the Israelites, as a visible sign of the sacrifice that had been performed. "Then they shall take some of the blood [of the lamb], and put it on the two doorposts and the lintel of the houses in which they eat them" (Exodus 12:7).

Although the Book of Exodus does not explicitly say how the lamb was killed, in ancient Israel, the usual method of sacrifice was to slit the animal's throat and drain the blood into a sacred vessel of some sort. The priest would then carry the blood to the altar and pour it out in sacrifice. This practice seems to lie behind Moses' more detailed commands regarding the blood of the lamb:

Then Moses called all the elders of Israel, and said to them, "Select lambs for yourselves according to your families, and kill the Passover lamb. *Take a bunch of hyssop and dip it in the blood which is in the basin, and touch the lintel and the two doorposts with the blood which is in the basin*; and none of you shall go out of the door of his house until morning. For the LORD will pass through to slay the Egyptians; and when he sees the blood on the lintel and on the two doorposts, the LORD will pass over the door, and will not allow the destroyer to enter your houses to slay you." (EXODUS 12:21–23)

Three things are worth noting here. First, the blood of the lamb was to be poured into a "basin." Intriguingly, although the Hebrew word can refer to a common basin (*saph*) for ordinary use, in sacrificial contexts it is more frequently a technical term for a sacred vessel, such as the "basins [*siphoth*] of silver" used in the Temple (2 Kings 12:14) for liquid offerings of blood, water, or wine. Second, the blood of the lamb was to be spread on the wood of the doorposts and lintels of each Israelite home, presumably because blood stains wood. In this way, the blood of the lamb would function as a permanent outward sign of the completed sacrifice, so that the destroying angel (and anyone else who happened to pass by) could see who had offered the sacrifice and who had not. Third and finally, this entire ritual was done using a branch of "hyssop," a strong wiry plant found in the Middle East whose bunches of flowers and leaves were good at absorbing liquid. This made it a perfect instrument for spreading the blood of the lamb on the wooden beams of the homes. As we will see later, the hyssop, the blood, and the wood will all reappear together when we come to Jesus' own Passover.

For now, the main point is that the ultimate goal of the Passover sacrifice—as well as its ultimate effect—was *deliverance from death through the blood of the lamb.* It was not just any kind of sacrifice; it was a sacrifice that had the power to save you from death.

Step 4: Eat the Flesh of the Lamb

The fourth step of the Passover sacrifice is, curiously, the one that is most often forgotten. And yet it is arguably the most important for understanding Jesus' actions at the Last Supper. After the lamb had been killed and its blood poured out and spread upon the entries of the homes, the Israelites would then eat the lamb:

> *They shall eat the flesh that night, roasted; with unleavened bread and bitter herbs they shall eat it.* Do not eat any of it raw or boiled with water, but roasted, its head with its legs and its inner parts. And you shall let none of it remain until the morning, anything that remains until the morning you shall burn. In this manner you shall eat it: your loins girded, your sandals on your feet, and your staff in your hand; and you shall eat it in haste. It is the LORD's Passover. For I will pass through the land of Egypt that night, and I will strike all the first-born in the land of Egypt, both man and beast. (EXODUS 12:8–12)

Again, while this part of the Passover is sometimes overshadowed by the dramatic and memorable act of spreading the blood, it was in fact equally (if not more) important. For example, if a certain Israelite family did not particularly care for the taste of lamb, what would have happened? If they took the lamb, sacrificed the lamb, spread the blood of the lamb, but did not eat the lamb, what would have been the result? Well, the Book of Exodus does not say. But it's a good guess that when they awoke the next morning, their firstborn son would be dead. For, as any ancient Jew would have known, *the Passover sacrifice was not completed by the death of the lamb, but by eating its flesh.* Five times the Bible states that they must "eat" the lamb; five times it emphasizes the sacrificial meal. The Passover was not completed by the death of the victim, but by a "communion" of sorts—by eating the flesh of the sacrifice that had been killed on your behalf.

And so the Israelites did. They ate "the flesh" of the Passover Lamb the same night it was killed, roasting it and consuming it with the unleavened bread and bitter herbs. The presence of the "unleavened bread" (Hebrew *matzah*) was a sign of the haste with which they left Egypt; there was no time to allow it to rise. In later Jewish tradition, the bitter herbs would come to symbolize the sufferings Israel endured in Egypt. With regard to the lamb, it could not be eaten raw or boiled, nor could it be cut into pieces. It had to be spitted with wooden rods, roasted whole over a fire, and eaten that night, with nothing left until morning. As some scholars have suggested, the Passover seems to have been a particular kind of sacrifice, known as a "thank offering," or, in Hebrew, a *todah* sacrifice (see Leviticus 7). It was an act of thanksgiving for deliverance from death.

Finally, it is worth noting that according to Exodus, the Passover was not an "open table" but a covenant feast. Only Israelites could eat of it. Any Gentile "foreigner"—

that is, a non-Israelite—who wanted to eat the flesh of the lamb first had to be circumcised and become a member of Israel (Exodus 12:43–49). In other words, this was no ordinary meal, but a sacred family ritual. Only members of the covenant family of God were able to partake of it.

Step 5: Keep the Passover as a "Day of Remembrance"

The fifth and final step was by no means the least significant. From the very beginning, the Passover sacrifice was not simply meant to be a one-time feast. Instead, it was designated as a memorial day, an annual celebration that was to be kept by Israel forever:

> This day shall be for you *a day of remembrance*; and you shall keep it as a feast to the LORD; throughout your generations you shall observe it as an ordinance forever. . . . (EXODUS 12:14)

> You shall observe this rite as an ordinance for you and your sons for ever. And when you come to the land which the LORD will give you, as he has promised, you shall keep this service. And when your children say to you, "What do you mean by this service?," you shall say, "It is the sacrifice of the LORD's Passover, for he passed over the houses of the people of Israel in Egypt, when he slew the Egyptians but spared our houses." And the people bowed their heads and worshiped. Then the people of Israel went and did so; as the LORD had commanded Moses and Aaron, so they did. (EXODUS 12:24–27)

Here we see that the final step was for the Passover liturgy to be repeated. Every year, in the spring, on the fourteenth day of the month of Nisan, Israel was to celebrate this "day of remembrance" in honor of the salvation that had been won for them by God through the hands of Moses (Exodus 13:1–10; Deuteronomy 16:1). This command to renew the sacrifice every year shows that for ancient Israel, Passover was not just a one-time event. It did not happen once and then pass away. The Passover was to be observed forever, until the end of time.

To sum up what we have seen so far, in the Old Testament itself, there are five basic steps of the ancient Passover. They are as follows:

> Step 1. Choose an unblemished male lamb.
> Step 2. Sacrifice the lamb.
> Step 3. Spread the blood of the lamb on the home
>   as a "sign" of the sacrifice.
> Step 4. Eat the flesh of the lamb with unleavened
>   bread.
> Step 5. Every year, keep the Passover as a "day of
>   remembrance" of the exodus forever.

This is the Passover of the exodus from Egypt. This is the biblical shape of the Passover liturgy, with which every ancient Israelite would have been familiar through reading the Scriptures and by celebrating the annual feast.

However, the first Passover was not identical to the Jewish Passover as celebrated at the time of Jesus. In addition to the Jewish Scripture, there is also Jewish tradition. By the first century A.D., the Jewish feast of Passover had developed both similarities and differences with the Passover of the exodus. So before looking at the Last Supper itself, we

need to also study these differences, so that we can understand Jesus' actions in their proper context.

WHAT WAS PASSOVER LIKE AT
THE TIME OF JESUS?

Over the fifteen or so centuries that passed between the
exodus from Egypt and the time of Jesus, the Jewish Passover developed and changed. This happens to most liturgical celebrations; over time, they expand, they contract,
some elements are added, others are taken away. With
regard to the Passover, certain steps, like the spreading of
the lamb's blood on the doorposts of the home, dropped
out. Other steps, such as the eating of the Passover lamb,
were kept, and their meanings were explained (and even
expanded) by later generations. Moreover, new rites and
rituals attached themselves to the Passover feast as it
changed with time, such as the drinking of cups of wine.

Because of the changing shape of the Passover, in
order to understand what it was like at the time of Jesus,
we need to look not only at the Old Testament but also
at ancient Jewish descriptions of the Passover outside the
Bible. In these writings, there are at least four key differences between the original Passover of Egypt and later
Jewish Passovers that merit our attention.

The Passover Sacrifice in the Temple

The first difference has to do with location. In the original Passover, the lambs were sacrificed and eaten in the
homes of the Israelites in Egypt. At the time of Jesus,

the lambs had to be sacrificed in the Temple and eaten in the city of Jerusalem. Moreover, in the original Passover, every Israelite father was able to offer sacrifice on behalf of his family. But at the time of Jesus, only the Levitical priests could pour out the blood of the lambs on the altar. This restriction of the Passover sacrifice to the Jerusalem Temple is laid down by God in the Torah:

> You may not offer the Passover sacrifice within any of your towns which the LORD your God gives you; but at the place which the LORD your God will choose, to make his name dwell in it, there you shall offer the Passover sacrifice, in the evening at the going down of the sun, at the time you came out of Egypt. And you shall boil it and eat it at the place which the LORD your God will choose. (DEUTERONOMY 16:5-7)

Two things stand out in this passage. First, it is clear that the Jewish Passover is not just a meal, but a "sacrifice" (Hebrew *zebah*). It is "the sacrifice of the LORD's Passover" (Exodus 12:27; Deuteronomy 16:5). Second, like every other blood sacrifice at the time of Jesus, the Passover lamb could only lawfully be offered in one place: the Temple in Jerusalem, where God had chosen to make his name dwell.

This link between the Passover and the Temple is important to emphasize. If you were a Jew living at the time of Jesus, in order to keep the Passover feast, you could not simply go down to the local market and buy a lamb to be killed and eaten privately in your own home. You first had to take the lamb to the *Temple* in Jerusalem and give it to an ordained *priest* to sacrifice it. It is for this reason that during Passover the city of Jerusalem would be brimming with Jewish pilgrims coming to the Temple to offer sacrifice. Fortunately, we don't have to imagine what this would have been like. In the writings of Josephus, we have an eyewitness account of this from Jesus' own day. Recall that Josephus was not only a historian, but a priest in the first century. In his history of the Jewish war, he gives us a detailed description of the number of sacrifices offered each year at Passover in the Temple:

> So these high priests, upon the coming of their feast which is called the Passover, when they slay their sacrifices, from the ninth hour [about 3 p.m.] to the eleventh [about 5 p.m.], but so that a company not less than ten belong to every sacrifice (for it is not lawful for them to feast singularly by themselves), and many of us are twenty in a company, found *the number of sacrifices was 256,500*; which, upon the allowance of no more than ten that feast together, amounts to 2,700,200 persons. (JOSEPHUS, *WAR* 6:423–27)

Even if somewhat exaggerated, this is a staggering figure: more than two hundred thousand lambs for some two million people! For the modern reader, who probably has never witnessed a single animal sacrifice, much less several thousand in one day, it is difficult to imagine just *how much blood* would have been poured out by the priests at Passover. But for ancient Jews, like Jesus and his disciples, who attended Passover every year of their adult lives, it would have been impossible to forget. No one living at the time of the Temple could have ever had any misconceptions about the fact that the first-century Passover was first a sacrifice and then a meal.

This sacrificial aspect of Passover at the time of Jesus is important to stress because modern people's concept of Passover is often shaped primarily by their knowledge of the contemporary Jewish Passover meal, known as the *Seder.* As we will see in Chapter 6, "The Fourth Cup and the Death of Jesus," the Seder certainly has ancient roots, as well as various parallels with the Passover meal as celebrated at the time of Jesus. However, one key way the modern Jewish Seder is fundamentally different from the first-century Jewish Passover is that *the Jewish Seder meal is not a Temple sacrifice.*

Historically, this difference is the result of the fact that, forty years after the death of Jesus (A.D. 70), the Roman army came and destroyed the Jerusalem Temple. From that day until our own, it has never been rebuilt. Because of this, all of the blood sacrifices commanded in the Mosaic Law have ceased. With the destruction of the Temple in the first century also came the end of a functioning Levitical priesthood, whose chief task was to offer sacrifice in the Temple. Without a Temple or an active priesthood, Judaism after A.D. 70 was forced to change. In the place of the Temple, the synagogue emerged as the primary place of Jewish worship. (The Greek word *synagoge* means "assembly" or "gathering place.") In the place of the Levitical priests, the rabbis emerged as the primary teachers of the Jewish people. (The Hebrew word *rabbi* means "my great one" or "my teacher.") Although synagogues and rabbis had certainly existed before the Temple's destruction—they are repeatedly spoken of in the Gospels—both were ultimately subordinate to the central sanctuary and its priests, where worship, according to the Mosaic Law, took the form of cultic sacrifice.

At the risk of being anachronistic, Judaism at the time of Jesus was much more like Catholicism (priests, leading worship centered on sacrifice), whereas rabbinic Judaism after the Temple's destruction was much more like Protestantism (Scripture teachers, leading worship without blood sacrifice). In short, because Jesus lived during the time of the Temple, when he celebrated the Passover, it would have involved a sacrifice led by a priest, not just a meal led by a layperson.

The Crucifixion of the Passover Lambs

The second difference between the first exodus and the Passover at the time of Jesus has to do with the *way* the Passover lamb was sacrificed in the Temple. Fascinatingly, we have evidence that, in the first century A.D., the Passover lambs in the Temple were not only sacrificed; they were, so to speak, *crucified*.

As the Israeli scholar Joseph Tabory has shown, according to the Mishnah, at the time when the Temple still stood, after the sacrifice of the lamb, the Jews would drive "thin smooth staves" of wood through the shoulders of the lamb in order to hang it and skin it (*Pesahim* 5:9). In addition to this first rod, they would also "thrust" a "skewer of pomegranate wood" through the Passover lamb "from its mouth to its buttocks" (*Pesahim* 7:1). As Tabory concludes, "An examination of the rabbinic evidence . . . seems to show that in Jerusalem the Jewish paschal lamb was offered in a manner which resembled a crucifixion." This conclusion is supported by the writings of Saint Justin Martyr, a Christian living in the mid–second century A.D. In his dialogue with a Jewish rabbi named Trypho, Justin states:

> For the lamb, which is roasted, is roasted and dressed up *in the form of a cross.* For one spit is

> transfixed right through from the lower parts up
> to the head, and one across the back, to which are
> attached the legs of the lamb. (JUSTIN MARTYR,
> *DIALOGUE WITH TRYPHO THE JEW*, 40)

If these descriptions of the Passover lambs in the Mishnah and Justin Martyr are accurate—and there is no good reason to doubt them—then on numerous occasions, Jesus himself would have witnessed the "crucifixions" of thousands of Passover lambs in the Jerusalem Temple. This is an aspect of the Passover in his day that is neither mentioned in the Bible nor part of the modern-day Jewish Seder, but which has the power to shed light on Jesus' conception of his own fate.

As we will see in a moment, Jesus is going to compare his suffering and death to the death of the Passover lamb. One reason he might have done this is that he expected that the manner of his death would resemble that of the lambs in the Temple. Not only would his lifeblood be poured out; but he, too, would be "crucified," his body transfixed to the wooden beams of a Roman cross, like many other Jews before him (compare Matthew 16:24).

A Participation in the First Passover

The third important difference between the original Passover and later Jewish tradition is that the ancient rabbis saw each annual celebration of the Passover as a way of participating in the first exodus. At the time of Jesus, the Passover was not just a sacrifice; it was also a "memorial" or "remembrance" (Exodus 12:14) by which the Jewish people would both remember and somehow *make present* the deliverance that had been won for their ancestors in the exodus from Egypt.

As the centuries passed, this double element of both remembering the past and making it present came to be expressed by various rituals recorded in ancient Jewish tradition. For example, according to the Mishnah, in the midst of the Passover meal, the son would ask the father, "Why is this night different from other nights?" and the father would answer by retelling the story of Abraham and the exodus (Mishnah, *Pesahim* 10:4). The father would also remember the exodus by explaining the meaning of the various parts of the Passover meal. He would tell how the "Passover" was a reminder of how God "passed over" the Israelites' houses, how the unleavened bread was a reminder of the redemption from Egypt, and how the bitter herbs were a memorial of the suffering of the enslaved people (Mishnah, *Pesahim* 10:5). All these together not only looked back to the original experience of deliverance but somehow made it present:

> *In every generation a man must so regard himself as if*
> *he came forth himself out of Egypt, for it is written . . .*
> *"It is because of what the Lord did for me when I came*
> *forth out of Egypt"* (Exod 13:8). Therefore we are
> bound to give thanks . . . and to bless him who
> wrought all these wonders for our fathers and for
> us. He brought us out from bondage to freedom,
> from sorrow to gladness, and from mourning to a
> Festival-day, and from darkness to great light, and
> from servitude to redemption; so let us say before
> him the Hallelujah. (MISHNAH, *PESAHIM* 10:5)

With these words, we see quite clearly that for ancient Jews, the Passover feast was not just a remembrance of what God had done for their ancestors. In some mysterious way, they saw each Passover, "in every generation," as a way of sharing in the original act of redemption. Although living centuries after the first exodus, the father would speak of the event as if it were something he himself had experienced.

In other words, ancient Jewish celebrants did not just remember the exodus; they actively *participated* in it. From their perspective, no matter how much time had passed since the days of Moses, the salvation won in the exodus was not just for "our fathers" but "for us." And the chief way both of remembering and of participating in the original act of redemption was, of course, by keeping the Passover itself.

The Passover of the Messiah

The final difference between the original Passover and Jewish tradition is that some traditions tied the Passover feast to the coming of the Messiah and the dawn of the age of salvation.

For example, in one ancient Jewish commentary on the Book of Exodus, Rabbi Joshua, son of Hananiah, who was of priestly descent and had served in the Temple before it was destroyed, says: "In that night they were redeemed, and in that night they will be redeemed" (*Mekilta* on Exodus 12.42). In other words, the future redemption will take place on the same night as the original redemption: Passover night. Along the same lines, in the ancient Jewish commentary the Midrash Rabbah, God says to his people: "On that very night"—that is, Passover night—"know that I will redeem you" (*Exodus Rabbah* 18:11). And again: "The Messiah who is called 'first,' will come in the first month" (*Exodus Rabbah* 12:42, alluding to Isaiah 41:27). The "first month" of the Jewish liturgical year was the month of Nisan, the month when the Passover was celebrated. All of these rabbinic traditions are apparently based on the fact that in the Bible, the night of Passover is called "a night of watching" (Exodus 12:42). The first Passover was a night of watching for the coming of the destroying angel. In later Jewish tradition, the Passover became a night of watching for the coming of the Messiah and the redemption he would bring.

Once again, we find evidence for an ancient Jewish belief in early Christian writings. Saint Jerome, who was arguably the greatest biblical scholar of the early Church (ca. A.D. 400), is well aware of the link between the Jewish Passover and the coming of the Messiah:

> It is a tradition of the Jews that the Messiah will come at midnight according to the manner of the time in Egypt when the Passover was (first) celebrated. (JEROME, *COMMENTARY ON MATTHEW* 4 ON 25:6).

In light of such Jewish and Christian evidence, the modern biblical scholar Joachim Jeremias has this to say about the Passover of the Messiah:

> The Jewish passover celebration at the time of Jesus is both retrospect and prospect. At this festival the people of God remember the merciful immunity granted to the houses marked with the blood of the paschal lamb and the deliverance from the Egyptian servitude. *At the same time the passover is a looking forward to the coming deliverance of which the deliverance from Egypt is the prototype.* This typology is a concept which "most comprehensively determined in early times, as no other did, the form that the doctrine of final salvation took." The Messiah comes in the Passover night!

The Messiah comes on Passover night, and God will redeem his people on that same night. With these ancient Jewish beliefs firmly in mind, we can now turn to Jesus' actions during his own final Passover meal, which he celebrated the night on which his passion began.

JESUS AND THE NEW PASSOVER

With all this in mind, we can now make some connections between the biblical Passover, ancient Jewish tradition, and Jesus' own words and deeds. If Jesus saw himself as inaugurating a new exodus, and if he expected the new exodus to be preceded by a new Passover, then when did he think this new Passover would take place? When we turn to the Gospels, there is really only one possible answer: at the Last Supper, when Jesus celebrated the final Passover of his life, immediately before his own "exodus," which he was to "accomplish at Jerusalem" (Luke 9:31).

As I suggested above, at the Last Supper, Jesus was not just keeping another annual memorial of the exodus from Egypt, important as that was. Instead, he was deliberately instituting a new Passover through which the new exodus would finally be set in motion. In order to see this clearly, we need to pay close attention to how the Last Supper was *similar* to other Jewish Passover meals, as well as how it was *different*. By focusing on these similarities and differences, we will see that Jesus was both keeping the old covenant Passover and, at the same time, fulfilling the Jewish expectation of a new Passover, the Passover of the Messiah.

The first similarity is the most basic: Jesus celebrated the Last Supper on Passover night, the very night the lambs were eaten by the Jewish people. Before describing the supper itself, the Gospels explicitly and repeatedly identify the Last Supper as a Jewish Passover meal:

> Now on the first day of Unleavened Bread the disciples came to Jesus, saying, "Where will you have us prepare for you *to eat the Passover?*" He said, "Go into the city to such a one, and say to him, 'The Teacher says, My time is at hand; *I will keep the Passover at your house* with my disciples.'" And the disciples did as Jesus had directed them, and *they prepared the Passover.* (MATTHEW 26:17–19)

> And on the first day of Unleavened Bread, *when they sacrificed the Passover lamb,* his disciples said to him, "Where will you have us go and prepare for you to eat the Passover?" (MARK 14:12)

> And when the hour came, he sat at table, and the apostles with him. And he said to them, "I have earnestly desired *to eat this Passover* with you before I suffer." (LUKE 22:14–15)

Here we see very clearly that Jesus' final supper took place immediately after the "sacrifice" of the Passover lambs, once the disciples had finished preparing the Upper Room for the celebration of the Passover (Greek *pascha*). The Gospel writers go to great pains to stress this point: as observant Jews, Jesus and his disciples kept the Passover feast the night before he died.

Second, for anyone familiar with the Jewish Passover meal, there are numerous similarities of detail that are fairly easy to spot. For example, Jesus and his disciples ate the Last Supper *in Jerusalem*, not in the town of Bethany where they had been staying (Mark 14:13; John 18:1). This fits with the Jewish tradition that the Passover had to be eaten within the city gates of Jerusalem. Jesus and the Twelve celebrated the Last Supper *at night*, something which was distinctive of the Passover meal, which was eaten "in the evening" (Deuteronomy 16:6). Moreover, Jesus and his disciples drank *wine* at the Last Supper, which was required for keeping the Jewish Passover, but different from the water usually drunk with ordinary meals (Mishnah, *Pesahim* 10:1). Perhaps most important of all, Jesus' act of *explaining the meaning of the bread* unquestionably points to the Passover. As we saw above, it was at Passover that the father of the house would answer his son's questions by explaining the meaning of the unleavened bread (Exodus 12:26–27; Mishnah, *Pesahim* 10:5). If this all wasn't enough, the Last Supper also ended with the *singing of a "hymn"* (Matthew 26:30; Mark 14:26). The mention of the hymn refers to Psalm 118, known as the "Great Hallel" psalm, which in Jewish tradition was sung toward the end of the Passover meal.

In addition to these similarities, the Last Supper was also different—radically different—from an ordinary Passover meal. Any ancient Jew, including the apostles, could easily have seen this. For one thing, most Passovers were celebrated within families, with the father leading and acting as head. At the Last Supper, by contrast, Jesus acted as host and leader of the Twelve, even though he was not the father of any of the disciples. Even more, at an ordinary Passover, the focus was on God's covenant with Abraham, the exodus from Egypt, and the entry into the promised land of Canaan. Yet Jesus spoke instead of the "new covenant," prophesied by Jeremiah to be fulfilled in the age of salvation (1 Corinthians 11:25; Jeremiah 31:31–33). Perhaps most significant, at an ordinary Jewish Passover, the entire liturgy revolved around the body and blood of the sacrificial Passover lamb. First, the lamb would be slaughtered, and the priests in the Temple would pour out the blood of the lamb on the altar. Then the Jews would bring the body of the lamb from the Temple to the Passover meal, and the father would explain its meaning at the meal. Yet, at the Last Supper, Jesus did something entirely different. With his words of explanation, he shifted the focus away from the body and blood of the Passover lamb (of which there is no mention), and turned it toward his own body and blood.

We can feel the force of this difference more if we compare Jesus' words at the Last Supper with other descriptions of the ancient Jewish Passover. For example, in its account of what the Passover was like when the Temple still stood, the Mishnah focuses on "the body" of the Passover lamb: "Rabbi Eliezer son of Rabbi Zadok says . . . And in the Holy Temple they used to bring before him *the body of the Passover offering*." (Mishnah, *Pesahim* 10:3–4)

Contrast this with what Jesus says at the Last Supper: "Now as they were eating, Jesus took bread, and blessed, and broke it, and gave it to the disciples and said, 'Take, eat; this is *my body*.'" (Matthew 26:26).

Along the same lines, before the Temple was destroyed, the climax of the Passover sacrifice was the pouring out of the lamb's blood by the priests in the Temple. The Mishnah again describes this in striking detail:

> The Passover-offering was slaughtered in three groups. . . . When the first group entered in and the Temple Court was filled, the gates of the Temple Court were closed. . . . The priests stood

in rows and in their hands were basins of silver
and basins of gold. In one row all the basins were
of silver and in another row all the basins were
of gold. . . . An Israelite slaughtered his offering
and the priest caught *the blood.* The priest passed
the basin to his fellow, and he to his fellow, each
receiving a full basin and giving back an empty
one. *The priest nearest to the Altar tossed the blood
in one action against the base.* . . . When the first
group went out the second group came in; and
when the second group went out the third group
came in. . . . [In the meantime] the Levites sang
the *Hallel.* If they finished it, they sang it anew.

(MISHNAH, *PESAHIM* 5:5–7)

The pouring out of the Passover blood must have been
a truly awesome sight, especially if some two hundred
thousand lambs were being sacrificed. Again, contrast the
rabbinic focus on the lambs' blood with what Jesus says at
the Last Supper:

And he took a cup, and when he had given thanks
he gave it to them, saying, "Drink of it, all of you;
for *this is my blood of the covenant, which is poured out
for many* for the forgiveness of sins." (MATTHEW
26:27–28)

When we compare Jesus' actions to these ancient Jewish traditions, it doesn't take much imagination to figure
out his point. By means of his words over the bread and
wine of the Last Supper, Jesus is saying in no uncertain
terms, *"I am the new Passover lamb of the new exodus. This is
the Passover of the Messiah, and I am the new sacrifice."*

If this interpretation is right, then the implications are enormous. For one thing, it shows that Jesus not only kept the Jewish Passover, he also deliberately altered it, thereby instituting a new Passover. As a Jewish man, he had celebrated Passover many times before; he knew full well what he was doing by changing it this time. He was showing that this was no ordinary Passover; it was the Passover of the Messiah, the night on which some Jews believed that Israel would at last be "redeemed" (*Exodus Rabbah* 18:11). That is why Jesus can say that *his* blood—not the blood of the Passover lamb—will be poured out for the forgiveness of sins.

A second sign that the Last Supper was a new Passover is Jesus' command for his actions to be repeated. When he told the disciples, "Do this in remembrance of me" (1 Corinthians 11:25), he was echoing the command of God to keep the ancient Passover as a "remembrance" forever (Exodus 12:14). By means of these words, he was commanding his disciples to perpetuate this new Passover sacrifice in the future. Although we might miss it, by means of this command, Jesus was in effect restoring the original priesthood of the twelve tribes of Israel. As any ancient Jew would have known, only the priests could "pour out" the blood (Matthew 26:27–28); yet that is precisely what Jesus commanded the Twelve disciples to do in memory of him. Significantly, although the sacrifice of the Passover lambs in the Temple ceased when the Romans destroyed Jerusalem in A.D. 70, the offering that Jesus commanded his disciples to do "in memory" of him continues to this day.

In short, by placing his own body and blood at the center of this new Passover, Jesus revealed that he saw himself as the new Passover lamb. As the great Lutheran scholar Joachim Jeremias said more than fifty years ago, by means of his actions in the Upper Room, Jesus was saying to his disciples, "I go to death as the true passover sacrifice." With these words, Jesus revealed that he saw himself as the unblemished male lamb that would be put to death so that others might live.

You Have to *Eat* the Lamb

With all of this in mind, we can now go back to our original question about the mystery of the Last Supper. How is it that Jesus, as an observant Jew, could have ever commanded his disciples to eat his body and drink his blood?

Part of the answer lies in who Jesus thought he was and what he thought would happen to him. When we study the Last Supper closely, we find that Jesus not only saw himself as the long-awaited Messiah, the "Son of Man" who would one day come on "the clouds of heaven" (Mark 14:61–62; Daniel 7:14). He also saw himself as *the new Passover lamb*, who would be sacrificed in order to inaugurate the new exodus, and whose blood would be poured out for the forgiveness of sins. Perhaps this is one reason why he not only expected to be executed, but to be crucified, just as the Passover lambs were crucified in the Jerusalem Temple. The reason Jesus' identification with the lamb matters is that, as we saw earlier, in both the Old Testament and ancient Jewish tradition, the sacrifice of the Passover lamb was not completed by its death. It was completed by a meal, by *eating the flesh of the lamb* that had been slain. Therefore, if Jesus saw himself as the new lamb, then it makes sense that he would speak of his blood being poured out and command the disciples to eat his flesh.

Of course, this immediately raises the question of

whether Jesus meant his words realistically or only symbolically. When he said the words "This *is* my body," did he mean only "This *represents* my body"? Or did he see the Last Supper as one of the last miracles he would perform, in which he actually transformed the bread and wine into his body and blood? Did he actually expect the disciples to eat his flesh, under the form of bread?

Endless battles have been waged over the meaning of the word "is" here, all to no avail. However, if we put Jesus' words *in context*, we can discover a possible solution. For the context of his words is quite clear: it is the Jewish *Passover.* Well, then, let's look again at the Passover. In the Old Testament, was it ever enough simply to sacrifice the lamb? No. Did the actual flesh of the lamb have to be eaten in order for the sacrifice to be complete? Yes. Could a *symbol* of the lamb's flesh suffice? By now, we know that the answer is negative.

In other words, Jesus knew full well what any first-century Jew would have known: when it came to the Passover, you did not only have to kill the lamb; in order to fulfill God's law, in order to be saved from death, you had to *eat* the lamb. As with the old Passover of the first exodus, so with the new Passover of the Messiah. The main difference between the two is that in the new Passover, the lamb is a *person*, and the blood of redemption is the blood of the Messiah.

Should there be any doubt about this link between Jesus' death as the lamb and the eating of his flesh at the Last Supper, it's important to remember that this is exactly how the first-century Eucharist was understood by one of the most Jewish of all early Christians: the apostle Paul. In his first letter to the Corinthians, Paul says:

> Christ *our Passover lamb* has been sacrificed. *Therefore, let us keep the feast!* (1 CORINTHIANS 5:7–8).

> The *cup of blessing* which we bless, is it not a com-
> munion in *the blood of Christ*? *The bread* which we
> break, is it not a communion in *the body of Christ*?
> (1 CORINTHIANS 10:16)

In both of these statements, Paul is referring to the Lord's Supper. In the first quotation, he not only identifies Jesus as the new "Passover lamb" who has been sacrificed. He also bases the celebration of the Eucharistic "feast" on Jesus' identity as the lamb. Perhaps this is why, in the second quotation, Paul can affirm without hesitation that the Eucharist is a real communion in the body and blood of Jesus. For Paul, who sees the Lord's Supper through Jewish eyes, it is nothing less than a new Passover. Christ "the Passover lamb" has been sacrificed; therefore, Christians must keep the new Passover "feast" of his body and blood.

In short, just as the ancient Jews saw their Passovers as a participation in the exodus from Egypt, so, too, Saint Paul and other early Christians saw the Eucharist as a real participation in both the Last Supper and the death of Jesus.

However, the Passover is not the only key that unlocks the mystery of the Last Supper. Nor does it answer every question we might ask. For one thing, if we grant that Jesus saw himself as the Passover lamb, how could he actually give his disciples his flesh to eat? Wouldn't this be cannibalism? And what about the Mosaic law against drinking blood? To be sure, the Passover lambs' blood was poured out on the altar, but it was never drunk. In order to answer these questions, we'll need to turn to the next chapter. For Jesus spoke of the Last Supper not only as a new Passover, but as the new manna from heaven.

4

---※ ※---

THE MANNA OF THE MESSIAH

Now that we've looked at the Last Supper through the lens of the new Passover, other questions begin to emerge. For example, if Jesus saw himself as inaugurating the new exodus, then *what food did he think would be given for the journey?*

Remember that in the Old Testament, the people of Israel did not go straight from Egypt to the promised land. Their journey took years of wandering in the desert—forty years, to be exact (Numbers 32:13). Known by ancient Jews as the "wilderness wandering," this journey was a time of great trial and tribulation. During those years, Israel's fidelity to their God was tested over and over again. And during that time in the desert, God sustained them on a daily basis by giving them a special food: the manna from heaven.

In this chapter, we will turn to our second key to

unlocking the mystery of Jesus and the Last Supper: the ancient Jewish expectation of new manna from heaven. As we will see, just as Jesus used beliefs about the Jewish Passover to reveal the sacrificial nature of the Last Supper, so, too, he used the hope for new manna—the manna of the Messiah—to reveal the supernatural nature of the Eucharist.

One reason this connection between the manna and the Last Supper is important to explore is that discussions of Jesus' Eucharistic teaching sometimes tend to revolve entirely around the Passover lamb. To be sure, the Passover is very important, as we've just seen. However, it is significant that when Jesus gave his most detailed teaching about what he was going to do at the Last Supper, he did not refer to the Passover lamb. Instead, he spoke of the manna of the exodus, the supernatural bread from heaven that God had given the Israelites in the desert (see John 6:35–59). Moreover, he also promised that he would give new manna to those who believed in him.

In order to see the importance of this new manna, we'll have to go back once again and study the original manna from heaven, in both the Old Testament and ancient Jewish tradition.

THE MANNA IN THE TABERNACLE

The story of the manna in the Old Testament is well known but also well worth reviewing. It can be found in Exodus 16, immediately after the unforgettable account of the crossing of the Red Sea. In that account, we read "Thus the LORD saved Israel that day from the hand of the Egyptians; and Israel saw the Egyptians dead upon the seashore. And Israel saw the great work which the LORD did against the Egyptians, and the people feared the LORD; and they believed in the LORD and in his servant Moses" (Exodus 14:30–31).

With the drowning of Pharaoh's horses and chariots, the departure from Egypt was officially complete. Pharaoh would seek them no more. Now began the difficult task of actually getting to the promised land. And no sooner had this task begun than the Israelites began to complain:

> And the whole congregation of the sons of Israel murmured against Moses and Aaron in the wilderness, and said to them, "Would that we had died by the hand of the LORD in the land of Egypt, when we sat by the fleshpots and ate bread to the full; for you have brought us out into this wilderness to kill this whole assembly with hunger." (EXODUS 16:2–3)

At first glance, this response seems difficult to believe. Just one chapter before, the Israelites had witnessed their deliverance by God in the waters of the Red Sea and sung the "Song of Moses" in thanksgiving (Exodus 15). Now, after being in the desert for just a short time, they begin to "murmur" against the very men who had delivered them. By doing this, they were in effect saying, "In Egypt, we may have had whips on our backs, but at least we had food in our bellies." The irony here is, of course, that according to the biblical account, the Israelites left Egypt with "very many cattle, both flocks and herds" (Exodus 12:38). Why not just eat some of them? Although we can only speculate, perhaps it was because the Israelites still saw these cattle as "gods," the very ones that they had worshiped (and thus refused to kill) during their stay in Egypt. Recall that it would not be long before they would make a golden *calf* out of their winnings and worship it as a god (Exodus 32). Apparently, God had gotten them out of Egypt; but he had not yet gotten Egypt out of them.

In any case, instead of responding to the Israelites' rebellion by destroying them, God performed a miracle and gave them a gift. Although the story of the manna is well known, we need to reread it carefully, paying close attention to certain elements that tend to be overlooked:

> Then the LORD said to Moses, "Behold, *I will rain down bread from heaven* for you; and the people shall go out and gather a day's portion every day, that I may test them, whether they will walk in my law or not. On the sixth day, when they prepare what they bring in, it will be twice as much as they gather daily . . ." And the LORD said to Moses, "I have heard the murmurings of the sons of Israel; say to them, '*At twilight you shall eat flesh, and in the morning you shall be filled with bread;* then you shall know that I am the LORD your God.'" In the evening quails came up and covered the camp; and in the morning dew lay round about the camp. And when the dew had gone up, there was on the face of the wilderness a fine, flake-like thing, fine as hoarfrost on the ground. When the sons of Israel saw it, they said to one another, "*What is it?*" For they did not know what it was. And Moses said to them, "*It is the bread which the LORD has given you to eat.*" (EXODUS 16:4–5, 11–15)

There are at least four qualities of the manna here that are important for us to highlight.

First, it should go without saying that, according to the Old Testament, the manna in the desert was no ordinary bread. It was *miraculous* "bread from heaven," given directly by God to his people for them to eat. The reason I even have to mention this is that in the last century or so, it has become very fashionable to identify the manna with a natural substance secreted by the tamarisk plant or by one of the desert insects that feeds on its leaves. This theory seems to have grown out of a distinctively modern skepticism toward miracles, not because of anything the Book of Exodus actually says. Unfortunately, the idea has become so widely known that many people no longer think of the manna as miraculous bread but as some kind of naturally generated "plant-goo."

However, if you read the biblical account closely, the miraculous nature of the manna is indisputable for at least four reasons. For one thing, it is called "bread from heaven," suggesting its supernatural origin. Even more important, no matter how much or how little manna the Israelites gathered, it always measured out an omer's worth (about a liter), and it never lasted more than a day (Exodus 16:16–20). To say the least, this is hardly the kind of thing that natural substances usually do. In addition, the Old Testament claims that the manna appeared every day for forty years, and that the miracle stopped when the Israelites got to the promised land (Joshua 5). This cannot be reconciled with the seasonal secretions of the tamarisk tree, which take place for only a couple of months in the summertime. Last but not least, the whole point of the story is that the Israelites "did not know what it was."

That's why they called it manna, from the Hebrew words meaning "What is it?" (*man hu*). If the biblical manna was just an ordinary phenomenon, its very name would make no sense.

Now, whether or not a modern reader actually *believes* that this kind of miracle is possible is somewhat beside the point. The point is that the Old Testament itself clearly describes a miracle, and Jesus read the Old Testament. He was no modern skeptic. Like other ancient Jews, he would have believed that the manna was not a merely natural substance but supernatural bread from heaven. He would have known the hymn from the Book of Psalms, which reads:

> [God] commanded the skies above,
>   and opened the doors of heaven;
> and he rained down upon them manna to eat,
>   and gave them the bread of heaven.
> Man ate *the bread of the angels;*
>   *he sent them food in abundance. . . .*
> And they ate and were well filled,
>   for he gave them what they craved.
>   (PSALM 78:23–25, 29)

Along the same lines, the Book of Wisdom says:

> Instead of these things you [God] gave your
>   people *the food of angels,*
> and without their toil you supplied them
>   from heaven with bread ready to eat,
> *providing every pleasure and suited to every taste.*
> From your sustenance manifested your sweetness
>   toward your children;

and the bread, ministering to the desire of the one
    who took it,
was changed to suit every one's liking.

    (WISDOM OF SOLOMON 16:20–21)

In short, according to the Old Testament, the manna
was nothing less than the *panis angelicus*, the "bread of
angels." It was bread from heaven, given by God, having
within it all sweetness.

Second, although it is often forgotten, the gift of the
manna was a double miracle. Not only did God give the
Israelites bread from heaven, he also gave them flesh from
heaven. In the morning, they ate the manna, but in the evening, they ate the flesh of the quail that covered the camp.
This, too, was miraculous. As the Lord says to Moses, "At
twilight you shall eat flesh, and in the morning you shall be
filled with bread; then you shall know that I am the LORD
your God" (Exodus 16:12). *Bread from heaven,* and *flesh from
heaven*—these were God's gifts to them. Again, the Book
of Psalms declares, "He rained flesh upon them like dust,
winged birds like the sand of the seas" (Psalm 78:27). This
double aspect will prove important momentarily, when
Jesus will speak of giving his disciples his own flesh to eat.

Third, the Israelites not only consumed the manna as their
daily food, they also preserved it, by *placing it in the Tabernacle.*
As we saw earlier, the Tabernacle was the portable temple in
which the Israelites worshiped God. Divided into three parts,
the Holy of Holies stood at its center, enshrining the golden
Ark of the Covenant. According to the Book of Exodus, God
commanded Moses to place some of the manna there:

"This is what the LORD has commanded: 'Let an
omer of [the manna] be kept throughout your

> generations that they may see the bread with which I fed you in the wilderness, when I brought you out of the land of Egypt.'" And Moses said to Aaron, "Take a jar, and put an omer of manna in it, and place it before the LORD, to be kept throughout your generations." As the LORD commanded Moses, so Aaron placed it before the covenant, to be kept. (EXODUS 16:32–34)

By means of this action, God was telling the Israelites that the manna was not only miraculous; it was holy. Indeed, it was most holy—so sacred that it was to be reserved in the Holy of Holies itself. Intriguingly, the purpose of reserving this manna was not so that the people might eat it, but so that they might look upon it. It was reserved so "that they may see the bread." According to the Book of Hebrews, this holy manna was kept "in a golden urn" in the Ark itself, alongside the tablets of the Ten Commandments and the staff of Aaron that budded (Hebrews 9:4). Clearly, for any ancient Jew, the manna was no ordinary bread.

Fourth and finally, but by no means least important, the manna of the exodus also had a distinctive flavor. As the Scripture says, "Now the house of Israel called its name manna; it was like coriander seed, white, and tasted like wafers made with honey" (Exodus 16:31).

Like "wafers made with honey"? Why did the manna taste like honey? The answer is simple, but important: it was *a foretaste of the promised land*—"the land flowing with milk and honey" (Exodus 3:8). In other words, by means of the manna, God was calling the Israelites to place their trust in his ability to provide for them and to see them home. He was in effect saying to them, "Trust me, be faithful to my commands, and I will bring you into the land promised to Abraham, Isaac, and Jacob."

Should there be any doubt about this connection between the manna and the promised land, it is important to remember that the manna was a temporary miracle. According to the Book of Joshua, as soon as the Israelites reached the promised land and were able to keep the Passover there, the manna ceased:

> While the sons of Israel were encamped in Gilgal [in the promised land] they kept the Passover on the fourteenth day of the month at evening in the plains of Jericho. And on the next day after the Passover, on that very day, they ate the produce of the land, unleavened cakes and parched grain. *And the manna ceased on the next day; and the sons of Israel had manna no more, but ate of the fruit of the land of Canaan.* (JOSHUA 5:10–12)

Why did the miracle stop? Once the exodus was complete, the manna was no longer necessary. Now that the Israelites were dwelling in the promised land, they no longer needed a pledge of God's faithfulness to bring them there. Now that the people had tasted the fruit of the land, they no longer needed the foretaste.

In short, when it comes to the exodus from Egypt, there are few things more memorable than the manna from heaven. According to the Old Testament, it was many things: miraculous bread from heaven, a sign of God's fidelity, and a foretaste of the promised land. And, in later Jewish tradition, it became one of the chief signs of what God would one day accomplish when he inaugurated the new exodus and sent the Messiah.

THE BREAD OF THE WORLD TO COME

When we turn to the place of the manna in ancient Jewish literature outside the Bible, we find a host of texts, far too many to study here. For the sake of understanding Jesus' teachings about the new manna from heaven, three ancient traditions stand out. First, some Jews believed that the manna given to the Israelites was not only miraculous but also "preexistent." It had actually existed before the Fall of Adam and Eve (Genesis 3). Second, another tradition held that the manna was a supernatural reality, kept on high in the heavenly Temple for the feeding of God's people. Third and finally, a widespread expectation existed that when the Messiah finally came, he would bring back the miracle of the manna. The manna that had stopped coming down during the time of Joshua would once again rain down from heaven. Before turning to Jesus' own words, we'll take a few moments to look at each of these in turn.

The Manna from the Beginning of Creation

Let's begin at the beginning. In several ancient Jewish writings, we find the belief that the manna from heaven was not just ancient history, but that it had existed from the very beginning of creation. For example, the Mishnah states that "the manna" was one of the "ten things" that was "created on the eve" of the seventh day of creation, the first Sabbath, along with the staff of Aaron that budded, and the tablets of the Ten Commandments (Mishnah, *Aboth* 5:6). Along the same lines, one ancient Jewish Targum—a translation of the Hebrew Scriptures used in the synagogue—adds this interesting element to its retelling of the Book of Exodus:

> And the Lord said to Moses, "Behold, I will bring down for you bread from heaven, *which has been reserved for you from the beginning.*" (*TARGUM PSEUDO-JONATHAN* ON EXODUS 16:4)

> When the children of Israel saw (it), they were amazed, and they said to one another, "What is it?" For they did not know what it was. And Moses said to them, "*It is the bread that was reserved for you from the beginning in the heavens on high;* and now the Lord is giving it to you to eat." (*TARGUM PSEUDO-JONATHAN* ON EXODUS 16:15)

Clearly, for some ancient Jews, the manna was not just a passing miracle, given to the Israelites during the exodus in order to make up for their lack of food. It was bread from the beginning of the world, from before the Fall of Adam and Eve. It had existed "on high" in heaven, before the entry of sin and death into human history.

In theological terms, this means some ancient rabbis believed that the manna was protological—that it had existed since the very dawn of creation. As such, the manna was the perfect food, untouched by the sin of humanity's first parents. In this way, for the rabbinic Judaism, the manna of the exodus was not just one more miracle but a kind of "return to Eden," a return to the state of creation before its corruption by sin and death. As we will see in a moment, both of these ideas will reappear in Jesus' sermon on the bread of life in the Jewish synagogue at Capernaum.

Eternal Bread in the Heavenly Temple

The second ancient Jewish tradition that is important for us is the belief that the manna was kept *in heaven*, within the heavenly Temple of God.

In order to understand this belief, it is important to remember that ancient Jews did not see reality like many modern people. In the contemporary Western world, we tend to reduce all of reality to the visible, material realm, what the rabbis would have called "this world" (*ha 'olam hazeh*). If modern people believe in a supernatural realm at all, we are often very vague or unsure about what it is like, and are hard-pressed to come up with a concrete description. In ancient Judaism, however, they saw the material world as a kind of visible sign of an invisible world, a supernatural realm in the heavens. At the center of this heavenly realm stood God himself, in his heavenly Temple, surrounded by myriads and myriads of angelic beings, those pure spirits who worshiped him night and day, for all time. Although these heavenly beings were not viewed as material realities, they were not for that reason any less "real." To the contrary, they were believed to be in a certain way more real than earthly things, which are temporary and therefore eventually pass away.

From this perspective, the earthly Temple in Jerusalem was a kind of visible, material sign (as Catholics might say, a "sacrament") of the invisible, immaterial dwelling of God, the heavenly Temple. According to the ancient rabbis, God and his angels were not the only residents in the heavenly Temple. The manna was there as well. Consider the commentary of the Jewish Talmud on the creation of the world in Genesis 1:

> "And God set them in the firmament of the heaven" (Gen 1:17). *"Skies" is that in which millstones*

stand and grind manna for the righteous for it is said:
"And He commanded the skies above, and opened
the doors of heaven; and He caused manna to rain
upon them for food" (Ps 78:23–24) etc. *"Habitation"*
is that in which [the heavenly] Jerusalem and the Temple
and the Altar are built, and Michael, the great Prince,
stands and offers up thereon an offering, for it is said:
"I have surely built Thee a house of habitation, a
place for thee to dwell in for ever" (1 Kgs 8:13).
And whence do we derive that it is called heaven?
For it is written: "Look down from heaven, and see,
even from Thy holy and glorious habitation" (Isa
63:15). (BABYLONIAN TALMUD, *HAGIGAH* 12B)

Unfortunately, the Hebrew wordplays in this passage
get lost in the English translation, making it a little compli-
cated. Nevertheless, the Jewish Talmud clearly teaches that
the manna was viewed as supernatural. Although eaten
by the righteous on earth, the manna was ground by the
angels "in heaven." This heavenly manna was believed to
be kept in the heavenly Temple, where Michael the arch-
angel himself served as chief celebrant at the altar of worship. As the modern Jewish scholar Rabbi R. Rabinowitz
says in his comments on this passage: "The earthly Temple
corresponds to the heavenly Sanctuary." In the Old Testament, as long as the Israelites had the Ark of the Covenant,
the manna was kept in the Holy of Holies, inside the earthly
sanctuary. But if the earthly Temple was a kind of copy or
image of a heavenly Temple, then it makes sense to suggest
that the earthly manna was likewise a kind of copy or image
of the heavenly manna, kept in the heavenly Temple.

In other words, just as some ancient Jews believed that
the Temple was an eternal reality that existed in heaven

long before it existed on earth, so, too, some Jews saw the manna as an eternal reality that existed in heaven long before it rained down to earth in the exodus from Egypt.

The Manna of the Messiah

The third Jewish tradition about the manna that is important for us flows directly from the second. Since the rabbis believed that the manna continued to exist in heaven, even after it had ceased on earth, many of them were waiting for the manna to return one day. And since they also believed that the Messiah would be a new Moses, many of them expected that the return of the manna would take place at the coming of the Messiah.

We'll cite just a few examples. According to the Midrash Rabbah, "As the first redeemer caused manna to descend, as it is stated, 'Because I shall cause to rain bread from heaven for you' (Exodus 16:4), so will the latter redeemer cause manna to descend" (*Ecclesiastes Rabbah* 1:9). In other words, just as the *first* Moses gave Israel manna from heaven, so too would the *new* Moses—the Messiah—bring down bread from heaven.

Another rabbinic commentary on Exodus states: "You will not find it [the manna] in this age, but you shall find it in the Age to Come" (*Mekilta* on Exodus 16:25). In Jewish tradition, "the Age to Come" (also translated as "the World to Come") was used to refer to the messianic age, when God would usher in the time of salvation for his people. At that time, they believed, the miracle of the manna would take place once again.

Finally, the oldest reference to the future manna is also the most detailed. In the ancient Jewish apocalypse known as *2 Baruch*, the author makes clear that the manna will return at the coming of the Messiah:

> And it will happen that when all that which should
> come to pass in these parts is accomplished, *the
> Messiah* will begin to be revealed. . . . And those
> who are hungry will enjoy themselves and they
> will, moreover, see marvels every day. . . . *And
> it will happen at that time that the treasury of manna
> will come down again from on high*, and they will eat
> of it in those years because these are they who
> will have arrived at the consummation of time.
>
> (2 *BARUCH* 29:3, 6–8)

This text, which most scholars date to the late first or early second century A.D., is an important witness to the fact that the Jewish belief in the return of the manna was circulating at the time of Jesus. It also shows that the coming manna was expected to be miraculous. In the days of Messiah, the righteous would see miracles ("marvels") every day, because they would eat the manna every day.

Finally, these expectations clearly link the future manna with the coming of the Messiah and the establishment of his kingdom on earth. As the New Testament scholar C. H. Dodd once put it, in these ancient Jewish traditions, the righteous will eat the manna during "the period of the temporary messianic kingdom on earth." In other words, the miracle of the manna belongs to the period between the coming of the Messiah (at the consummation of time) and the final resurrection of the dead and the restoration of creation. Just as the Israelites ate the manna after they left Egypt but before they got to the promised land, so, too, would the righteous eat the manna *after* the coming of the Messiah but *before* the final judgment at the end of human history.

In short, ancient Jewish tradition bears witness to a

vibrant hope that the miraculous manna of Moses would one day come again, and that the Messiah himself would bring it. When the new exodus finally began, God would strengthen his people as he had in the days of old by once again raining down bread from heaven. This would happen every day, so that the people of God might have a foretaste of the new promised land of the new creation— what some rabbis called "the Bread of the World to Come" (*Genesis Rabbah* 82:8).

JESUS AND THE NEW MANNA

With this background in mind, we can ask these questions: Did Jesus ever refer to the ancient Jewish hope for the new manna from heaven? And did he ever use this belief to shed light on the mystery of the Last Supper?

According to the Gospels, he did in fact do so on at least two occasions. First, although it is sometimes missed, there is a fleeting but important reference to the new manna in the Lord's Prayer, the one prayer that Jesus is recorded as having taught his disciples (Matthew 6:9–13; Luke 11:2–4). Second, there is Jesus' famous "Bread of Life" discourse, which took place in the Jewish synagogue at Capernaum (John 6:48–71). In that sermon, Jesus repeatedly referred to the manna from heaven, using it to explain to his disciples how they would be able to eat his flesh and drink his blood. Indeed, this sermon in the synagogue is Jesus' most detailed discussion of the Eucharist in all four Gospels. As a result, it will take us a few moments to unpack. However, as I hope to show, it is well worth our attention (not least because it is the passage that first led me to study this subject, and ultimately, to write this book).

But first, let's look at the Lord's Prayer.

"Give Us This Day Our Supernatural Bread"

Perhaps no words of Jesus are more well known than those found in the Lord's Prayer, also known as the "Our Father." These words are recorded in two places in the Gospels (Matthew 6:9–13; Luke 11:1–4), but their most familiar form is from the first Gospel:

> Our Father who art in heaven,
> Hallowed be thy name.
> Thy kingdom come.
> Thy will be done, on earth as it is in heaven.
> *Give us this day our daily bread;*
> And forgive us our trespasses, as we forgive
>   those who trespass against us.
> And lead us not into temptation, but deliver
>   us from evil.
>
> (MATTHEW 6:9–13)

Although we could say a lot about the Lord's Prayer as a whole, given our focus on the manna, we only need to ask two sets of questions: First, what is the object of the fourth petition, "Give us this day our daily bread"? What exactly was Jesus teaching the disciples to pray for? Was he simply telling them to pray for daily sustenance, to ask God the Father for ordinary food and drink? Or is something more going on here? Second, why did Jesus repeat himself in this line? Why not just say "Give us our daily bread" or "Give us this day our bread"? Why the redundancy? Why emphasize the *daily* nature of the bread the disciples are to ask for?

It seems to me that the answer to these questions lies in the mysterious Greek word *epiousios*, which is used in this line of the prayer. Although most English versions translate this line as if the word "day" or "daily" occurred twice, in fact, it does not. The normal word for "day" in Greek is *hemera*. Behind the English word "daily" lies another word, found in both versions of the "Our Father."

"Give us this day our *epiousios* bread."
(MATTHEW 6:11)

"Give us each day our *epiousios* bread."
(LUKE 11:3)

What is the meaning of this word? What is this *epiousios* bread? Unfortunately for modern scholars, our ability to answer this question is plagued by two difficulties. First, we have no way of knowing if the Greek word *epiousios* is a translation of an original Hebrew or Aramaic expression, and, if so, exactly what that expression was. In light of this situation—as with most of the words of Jesus—the actual Greek text is probably as far back as we can reasonably go. Second, the word *epiousios* is what scholars call a neologism (a "new word"). It occurs for the first time in ancient Greek literature right here in the Lord's Prayer. In later centuries, it will make its way into the writings of the early Church Fathers, but the word ultimately comes from the New Testament. This makes it difficult to be certain exactly what the word meant in its original context.

For these reasons, scholars continue to debate the meaning of *epiousios* in the Lord's Prayer, and have proposed a number of different translations. Some suggest that the word means "for the current time" (*epi ten ousan*). Others suggest that it means bread "for the coming" day (*he epiousa*). Both of these would be appealing, except that they aren't what the Greek text actually says. Others suggest that the word means bread "for existence" (*epi ousia*). This is the best guess so far, since it is closest to the Greek, and has some strong advocates.

However, I would argue that the most accurate (and ancient) translation is the one most often overlooked. If we break up the word into its two main parts and just translate it literally, this is what we find: (1) *epi* means "on, upon, or above," and (2) *ousia* means "being, substance, or nature." Put these two together and the meaning seems to be: "Give us this day our *supernatural* bread." Indeed, among some ancient Christian writers, it was very common to translate the Greek word *epiousios* as literally as possible. In perhaps the most famous translation of the Lord's Prayer ever made, in the fourth-century Latin Vulgate, Saint Jerome writes these words:

> Give us this day our *supersubstantial* bread.
>
> (MATTHEW 6:11)

What is the meaning of Jerome's translation? He himself tells us elsewhere: the bread of the Lord's Prayer is supersubstantial because "it is above all substances and surpasses all creatures." In other words, it is supernatural. And Jerome is not alone in this understanding. Significantly, Saint Cyril, bishop of Jerusalem in the fourth century A.D., also says of the Lord's Prayer: "Common bread is not supersubstantial, but this Holy Bread is supersubstantial" (*Mystagogic Lectures*, 23.15). Likewise, Saint Cyprian of Carthage, writing in the third century A.D., says in his treatise on the Lord's Prayer that the bread Jesus speaks of is "heavenly bread," the "food of salvation."

At this point you might be thinking, It's all Greek to me! But it's also all very important. If Jerome was right and the "Our Father" is a daily prayer for supernatural bread, then in a first-century Jewish context, it can only be referring to one thing: the new manna from heaven. While modern ears may miss the echoes of the Old Testament, any ancient Jew who heard a prayer for bread that was both *daily* and *supernatural* would have immediately thought of the manna of the exodus. This is especially true if the prayer for daily supernatural bread also mentioned the final coming of the "kingdom" of God (Matthew 6:10). Remember, on another occasion, Jesus commanded his disciples *not* to worry about earthly food—"what you shall eat" or "what you shall drink"—but to seek first the kingdom of heaven (Matthew 6:25–33; Luke 12:22–31). If everything else in the Lord's Prayer is focused on things spiritual, things "in heaven," then it makes good sense to say the same of the mysterious *epiousios* bread.

In sum, the hope for the new manna from heaven stands at the very center of the Lord's Prayer, the one prayer that we know Jesus taught to his disciples. Before his disciples were to ask for anything else for themselves— the forgiveness of their trespasses, protection from temptation, or deliverance from evil—they were to ask first for the new manna of the new exodus, the supersubstantial daily bread. By instructing his disciples to say each day, "Give us this day our supernatural bread," Jesus taught them to ask God for the miraculous food that the Messiah himself would give them during their journey to the new promised land. As the Anglican New Testament scholar N. T. Wright put it in his comments on the Lord's Prayer:

> Manna was not needed in Egypt. Nor would it be needed in the promised land. It is the food of inaugurated eschatology, the food that is needed because the kingdom has already broken in and because it is not yet consummated. The daily provision of manna signals that the Exodus has begun, but also that we are not yet living in the land.

It should go without saying that if this was the meaning Jesus intended for the "Our Father," then he saw himself as the Jewish Messiah who would once again rain down the new manna from heaven.

Jesus' Bread of Life Sermon in the Synagogue

By far the most explicit reference to the Jewish hope for the new manna occurs in one of Jesus' most famous and most controversial teachings: the so-called bread of life discourse (John 6:35–58). According to the Fourth Gospel, this teaching was given in the synagogue at Capernaum, a small village in Galilee. Anyone familiar with the centuries-old debate over how Jesus understood the Last Supper also knows that this particular sermon stands at the very heart of the controversy. For this is where he uttered the words with which we began our investigation:

> Amen, amen, I say to you, unless you eat the flesh of the Son of Man and drink his blood, you have no life in you; he who eats my flesh and drinks

my blood has eternal life, and I will raise him up
at the last day. For my flesh is real food and my
blood is real drink. (JOHN 6:53–55)

What could Jesus possibly have meant by saying such
things? Was he speaking literally, or only symbolically?
How did he think he was able to give others his flesh and
blood to eat and drink?

In order to answer these questions, we need to not only
pay close attention to the words of Jesus but also to interpret those words in their original context. When we do
this, we discover something very important: namely, *the
whole context of Jesus' bread of life discourse is centered on the Jewish hopes for the coming of a new Moses and the return of the
manna from heaven.*

It is remarkable how consistently this is overlooked in the
endless debate over Jesus' view of the Eucharist. And yet it
is true. For example, if you go back and read Jesus' bread
of life sermon in its broader context, you'll find that the
chapter *begins* with his miraculous feeding of five thousand
people in the desert (John 6:1–15). You don't have to be a
biblical scholar to draw a connection between Moses, who
once fed the Israelites with manna, and Jesus, who now feeds
the crowds with bread. Sure enough, in response to the miracle, the Jews themselves did two things. First, they recognized Jesus as Messiah. As the Gospel tells us, Jesus withdrew
from them because they were going to "take him by force
and make him king" (John 6:15). Second, they also identified Jesus as *a new Moses.* That is the meaning of their cry
"This is indeed the prophet who is to come into the world!"
(John 6:14). They are referring to the biblical "prophet like
Moses," as foretold in the Book of Deuteronomy.

In fact, if we read a little further in John 6, we find that the people's proclamation of Jesus as the new Moses leads straight into the bread of life discourse. As the Gospel tells us, after the people experienced the miracle, they came seeking Jesus and demanding that he perform another sign. Guess what they demanded of him? To bring down the manna from heaven:

> So they said to him, "Then what sign do you do, that we may see, and believe you? What work do you perform? *Our fathers ate the manna in the wilderness; as it is written, 'He gave them bread from heaven to eat.'*" Jesus then said to them, "Amen, Amen, I say to you, it was not Moses who gave you the bread from heaven; my Father gives you the true bread from heaven. For the bread of God is that which comes down from heaven, and gives life to the world." They said to him, "*Lord, give us this bread always.*" (JOHN 6:30–34)

Given what we've learned in this chapter about the Jewish hope for the new manna, this scene makes perfect sense in its historical context. The Jewish crowds knew that the Messiah was supposed to be a new Moses. They also knew that he was supposed to bring back the miracle of the manna. So, in order to test Jesus and see if he was in fact the one, they asked him to establish his messianic pedigree by performing a miracle. They challenged him to give them the new manna from heaven, with one twist. They wanted him to do so not just for forty years, like the old manna, but for *always*.

This request for the manna of the Messiah is what prompts Jesus to launch into the bread of life discourse proper, one of his longest teachings in the Fourth Gospel

(John 6:35–59). Instead of dissecting the entire sermon, I want to focus here on the part that contains Jesus' most explicit teaching on his real presence in the food and drink of the Last Supper (John 6:48–58). This section is not only the climax of Jesus' sermon in the synagogue; it is also one of the most important scriptures we will study in this book. So we need to look at it closely.

Jesus begins the sermon by using the manna to reveal his heavenly origin and the importance of believing in him (John 6:35–47). As soon as he has done this, he shifts his emphasis to the importance of eating his flesh. In these verses, notice how prominent are his references to the biblical manna:

> [Jesus said:] "I am the bread of life. *Your fathers ate the manna in the wilderness, and they died. This is the bread which comes down from heaven, that a man may eat of it and not die.* I am the living bread which came down from heaven; if any one eats of this bread, he will live for ever; and *the bread which I shall give for the life of the world is my flesh.*"
>
> The Jews then disputed among themselves, saying, "How can this man give us his flesh to eat?" So Jesus said to them, "Amen, Amen, I say to you, unless you eat the flesh of the Son of Man and drink his blood, you have no life in you; he who eats my flesh and drinks my blood has eternal life, and I will raise him up on the last day. *For my flesh is real food, and my blood is real drink.* He who eats my flesh and drinks my blood abides in me, and I in him. As the living Father sent me, and I live because of the Father, so he who eats me will live because of me. *This is the bread which came down from heaven, not such*

as the fathers ate and died; he who eats this bread will live forever." This he said in the synagogue, as he taught at Capernaum. (JOHN 6:48–59)

It is widely recognized by New Testament scholars—Protestant and Catholic alike—that Jesus is speaking here about the Eucharistic food and drink that he will give the disciples at the Last Supper. For one thing, he explicitly says that his flesh and blood are "real food" and "real drink" (John 6:55). Moreover, as the Lutheran scholar Joachim Jeremias points out, there are striking parallels between the two events:

Bread of Life Discourse	*The Last Supper*
The bread which I will give	This
is my flesh	is my body
for the life of the world	which is for you
(John 6:51)	(1 Corinthians 11:24)

In light of such parallels, which can hardly be coincidental, any attempt to insist that Jesus was not speaking about what he would do at the Last Supper here is a weak case of special pleading.

The question remains, however, what did Jesus actually *mean* when he said it was necessary to eat his flesh and drink his blood? Was he speaking literally, symbolically, or in some other manner? Granted he was speaking about what he would do at the Last Supper, did he mean what he said?

It is here that I think paying close attention to how Jesus used ancient Jewish beliefs about the manna can help us answer the question. Although many commentators recognize he was talking about the Last Supper, something important often goes unnoticed. *When Jesus gave his most*

explicit teaching on his real presence in the Eucharist, he directly
identified it with the new manna from heaven.

Look back at the second part of the sermon. Jesus
began it by saying, "Your fathers ate the manna in the
wilderness" (John 6:48). He ended it by contrasting the
Eucharist with the old manna: "This is the bread that
comes down from heaven, not such as the fathers ate and
died; he who eats this bread will live forever" (John 6:58).
In other words, Jesus surrounded his teaching about the
mystery of his presence in the Eucharist with references
to the manna from heaven. This is extremely significant.
Jesus could have chosen the Passover lamb to explain
the Eucharist, or (as we will see in the next chapter) the
mysterious Bread of the Presence. But when he wanted to
emphasize the necessity of eating his flesh and drinking
his blood and the fact that it would somehow become "real
food" and "real drink," he didn't choose either of these.
He used the Jewish hope for new bread from heaven, and
identified the Eucharist with the manna of the Messiah.

How does this help to solve the problem of what he
meant? It's actually rather simple, if you look at it through
ancient Jewish eyes. From a Jewish perspective, if the
Eucharist of Jesus is the new manna from heaven, then
it can't be just a symbol. It must be supernatural bread
from heaven. As we saw above, in the Old Testament, the
old manna of the exodus was no ordinary bread; it was
miraculous. That's why the Israelites put it in the Tabernacle with the other miraculous objects: Aaron's rod that
budded and the Ten Commandments, written with "the
finger of God" (Hebrews 9:4). Again, the Israelites had
never seen anything like the manna before. That's why
they called it "the bread of angels" (Psalm 78:25). And
that's also why later Jewish tradition believed that the

manna was a heavenly reality, which existed before the Fall of Adam and Eve and was kept in the heavenly Temple until the coming of the Messiah.

Now let's ask a pivotal question: If a first-century Jew believed that the old manna was supernatural bread from heaven, then could the new manna be just a symbol? If the old manna was the miraculous "food of the angels," could the new manna be just ordinary bread and wine? If so, that would make the old manna *greater* than the new! But that is not how salvation history works in the Bible. Old Testament prefigurations (known as types) are never greater than their New Testament fulfillments (known as antitypes). In Scripture, King David prefigured Jesus; David was called the royal "son of God" (Psalm 2). But David was not greater than Jesus—remember that little incident with Bathsheba? Likewise, King Solomon also was a type of Jesus; he was the wise king, the maker of many "parables" (1 Kings 4). But again, Solomon was not greater than Jesus—remember those four hundred wives and three hundred concubines? As Jesus himself says in the Gospels, "Behold, something greater than Solomon is here" (Matthew 12:42). Again he says, the Messiah is David's "Lord," and not just his "son" (Mark 12:36–37).

In short, *if the old manna of the first exodus was supernatural bread from heaven, then the new manna of the Messiah must also be supernatural bread from heaven.* This is of course exactly what Jesus said in the synagogue at Capernaum. After identifying the new manna as his own "flesh" (John 6:51), he ended by declaring, "This is the bread which came down from heaven, not such as the fathers ate and died; he who eats this bread will live for ever" (John 6:58). This is a striking statement. The only other reference in the Jewish Bible to being able to "eat and live for ever" refers to the fruit of the Tree of Life, from which Adam and Eve were driven out (Genesis 3:22). Could Jesus have been drawing on the ancient Jewish tradition that the manna had existed before the Fall? We can't be sure. But one thing is certain. If Jesus had wanted his Jewish disciples to regard the Eucharist as ordinary food and drink, he would certainly never have identified it as the new manna from heaven.

"This Is a Hard Saying"

As we bring this chapter to a close, I think it's important to address one last issue that may be lingering in the mind of the reader. That is the question of *how*. Even if we take Jesus at his word, how is it possible for him to actually give his disciples his flesh to eat? Did he intend for them to engage in cannibalism? And what about the prohibition against drinking animal blood in Leviticus? Was Jesus breaking the Law of God by commanding his disciples to drink his blood? Last, but certainly not least, what about the apparent audacity of claiming that he could even do such a thing? How could a mere man give himself in this way to others, much less teach that their salvation was somehow dependent upon consuming his flesh and blood?

The answer to these questions can be found by paying close attention to how the disciples reacted to his sermon on the new manna and how Jesus responded in turn to their reaction. If we want to know how to interpret Jesus' words in their historical context, we need to look at how he was understood by his first disciples. Remember, the disciples themselves were all Jews. How did they react to his teaching? Not too well, as John tells us in the very next verses:

Many of his disciples, when they heard it, said, "This is a hard saying; who can listen to it?" But Jesus, knowing in himself that his disciples murmured at it, said to them, "Do you take offense at this? Then what if you were to see the Son of man ascending to where he was before? It is the Spirit that gives life, the flesh is of no avail; the words that I have spoken to you are Spirit and life. But there are some of you that do not believe." For Jesus knew from the first who those were that did not believe, and who it was that would betray him. And he said, "This is why I told you that no one can come to me unless it is granted him by the Father."

After this many of his disciples drew back and no longer walked with him. Jesus said to the Twelve, "Will you also go away?" Simon Peter answered him, "Lord, to whom shall we go? You have the words of eternal life; and we have believed, and have come to know, that you are the Holy One of God." (JOHN 6:60–69)

First and foremost, we must emphasize the negative reaction of many of Jesus' disciples to his Eucharistic words. It is very hard to overestimate the importance of their response. Like the other Jews in the synagogue, *Jesus' disciples took him literally*. They "took offense" at his words, decided to leave his company, and he let them go.

This is extremely revealing for a number of reasons. For one thing, it gives us firsthand testimony to how Jesus' words would have sounded to actual first-century Jews. His insistence that they eat his flesh and drink his blood in the form of food and drink was so shocking to their Jewish ears that they could barely stand to hear it. "This is a

hard saying; who can listen to it?" (John 6:60), they said.
Like the Israelites in the desert who murmured about the
manna (Exodus 16:2–9), Jesus' followers "murmured" at
his difficult and distressing claims. In other words, they
didn't believe him. As Jesus said to them, "There are some
of you who don't believe" (John 6:64).

Moreover, notice exactly what the disciples' dilemma
was, and what it wasn't. The difficulty was *not* that they
misunderstood Jesus by taking him too literally. This had
happened before, and when it did, Jesus would clarify or
explain himself. For example, on another occasion, when
the disciples took Jesus' words too literally, he explained
his teaching as a metaphor:

> When the disciples reached the other side [of the
> lake], they had forgotten to bring any bread. Jesus
> said to them, "Take heed and beware of the leaven
> of the Pharisees and Sadducees." And they dis-
> cussed it among themselves, saying, "We brought
> no bread." But Jesus, aware of this, said, "O men of
> little faith, why do you discuss among yourselves
> the fact that you have no bread? Do you not yet
> perceive? . . . How is it that you fail to perceive
> that I did not speak about bread? Beware of the
> leaven of the Pharisees and Sadducees." Then they
> understood that he did not tell them to beware
> of the leaven of bread, but of the teaching of the
> Pharisees and Sadducees. (MATTHEW 16:5–12)

Contrast this response with Jesus' Eucharistic discourse. After the disciples objected to the bread of life
sermon, Jesus did not say to them, "Do you not perceive
or understand?" (Mark 8:17). What he said was, "Do you

take offense at this?" (John 6:61). In other words, with regard to Jesus' Eucharistic teaching, his disciples' primary problem was not that they didn't understand him. Their problem was that they didn't believe him.

Because of this, something shocking happens. In the wake of his bread of life sermon, *many of Jesus' followers abandoned him, and he let them go.* As the Gospel tells us, "After this, many of his disciples drew back and no longer walked with him," meaning that they stopped being his followers (John 6:66). This is extraordinary; it's the only time in all four Gospels that Jesus was ever abandoned by his own followers because of something he taught. And why did they leave? Because they took his Eucharistic teaching literally. But did he back down? No.

In fact, not only did Jesus let his disbelieving disciples go, but he turned to Peter and the Twelve and invited them to leave, too: "Will you also go away?" (John 6:67). The point is clear: Jesus would brook no compromise on the mystery of his body and blood. It was a litmus test of discipleship. And how did Peter respond to this test? As spokesman for the Twelve, he said, "Lord, to whom shall we go? You have the words of eternal life, and we have come to believe that you are the Holy One of God" (John 6:68–69). Essentially, Peter was saying, "Lord, I don't fully grasp *what* you just said, but I do know *who* you are."

Again, Jesus' Eucharistic teaching was not like the allegorical Parable of the Sower, where the disciples just needed some explaining. His shocking words about eating his flesh and drinking his blood called for supernatural faith. That is what Jesus meant when he said to those who didn't believe him: "No one can come to me unless it is granted him by the Father" (John 6:65).

But this isn't where the story ends. In Jesus' response

to the disciples' disbelief, *he also gave them the keys to under-standing his mysterious words.* I cannot stress this point enough. According to the Gospel, Jesus did not leave his befuddled disciples entirely in the dark. Reread his words very carefully:

> Jesus, knowing in himself that his disciples murmured at it, said to them, "Do you take offense at this? *Then what if you were to see the Son of man ascending to where he was before? It is the Spirit that gives life, the flesh is of no avail; the words that I have spoken to you are Spirit and life.* But there are some of you that do not believe." For Jesus knew from the first who those were that did not believe, and who it was that should betray him. (JOHN 6:62–64)

In this response, Jesus gave the Twelve disciples two clues to help them grasp the meaning of his difficult words: (1) the mystery of his divine identity; and (2) the mystery of his bodily resurrection and ascension, through the power of the Spirit. Let's take a few moments to look at these two.

The First Key: The Mystery of Jesus' Divine Identity

The first of these two keys is critically important. One very good objection to a realistic interpretation of Jesus' Eucharistic words is that no mere man could ever even have the power to give his body and blood to others, without them cannibalizing his corpse. Moreover, the audacity of any such man—be he prophet or not—declaring it necessary for others to eat his flesh and drink his blood in order that they might have eternal life, is staggering. Such a person, to echo the famous words of C. S. Lewis, is either a liar, a lunatic, or the Lord himself. But this is precisely why, in Jesus' response to the disciples' unbelief, he points first of all to his identity as a heavenly Messiah: "What if you were to see the Son of Man *ascending to where he was before?*" (John 6:62).

This is neither the first nor the only time that this happened. On more than one occasion, in both the Synoptic Gospels and in John, Jesus said things that burst the boundaries of ordinary human nature, making claims that could be justified only by the mystery of his divine identity. To take but a few examples: Once, in the city of Capernaum, Jesus said to a paralyzed man, "My son, your sins are forgiven you." To this, the Jewish scribes who were sitting nearby rightly objected: "Why does this man speak thus? It is blasphemy! Who can forgive sins but *God alone?*" To their objection, Jesus responded, "The Son of Man has authority on earth to forgive sins" (Mark 2:5–10), thereby claiming a divine prerogative as his own.

On another occasion, when questioned about why his disciples were doing something the Pharisees considered impermissible on the Sabbath, Jesus fired back at his critics: "*Something greater than the Temple is here,*" and "The Son of Man is *Lord of the Sabbath*" (Matthew 12:6–8). This is astonishing. From a Jewish perspective, the Temple was nothing less than the dwelling place of God on earth. What could possibly be "greater than the Temple" but God himself? And again, how could Jesus claim that the Son of Man (with whom he repeatedly identifies himself) is the "Lord of the Sabbath"? From a Jewish perspective, there can be only *one* Lord of the Sabbath: the one who made the Sabbath, God the creator.

In yet another encounter, Jesus said to his opponents:

"Amen, amen, I say to you *before Abraham was, I AM* [Greek *ego eimi*]" (John 8:58). With these words, he went so far as to claim as his own the divine name that had been revealed to Moses (see Exodus 3:14). It's no wonder that he almost got himself stoned to death as a result.

Last, but certainly not least, consider the shocking statements of Jesus in the Jewish Temple during the feast of Hannukah:

> It was the feast of Dedication at Jerusalem; it was winter, and Jesus was walking in the Temple, in the portico of Solomon. So the Jews gathered round him and said to him, "How long will you keep us in suspense? If you are the Messiah, tell us plainly." Jesus answered them, "I told you, and you do not believe; the works that I do in my Father's name, they bear witness to me . . . *I and the Father are one.*" The Jews then took up stones again to stone him. Jesus answered them, "I have shown you many good works from the Father; for which of these do you stone me?" The Jews answered him, "*We stone you for no good work but for blasphemy; because you, being a man, make yourself God.*" (JOHN 10:22–33)

Once again, Jesus' Jewish listeners understood him quite well. By claiming to be one with God the Father, he was doing nothing less than making himself God. And if his claims were false, then this was indeed blasphemy, the breaking of one of the Ten Commandments.

In other words, what I'm driving at, and what I think Jesus was driving at, is that you really cannot understand his claims about the Eucharist without first grasping his claims about his divine identity. You cannot understand how he, as Son of Man, can give his body and blood as food and drink, unless you understand that he, as Son of Man, has divine power: he is greater than the Temple, he is the Lord of the Sabbath, he is the one who bears the very name of God. That's why in his response to the disciples' disbelief, Jesus pointed first of all to his *identity* as the heavenly Son of Man, who existed before the world was made: "What if you were to see the Son of Man ascending to where he was before?" (John 6:62). It is only through the mystery of Jesus' divine identity and divine power that he will be able to give his disciples his body and blood under the form of "real food" and "real drink" (John 6:55).

The Second Key: The Mystery of the Resurrection

The second key to understanding is equally important, and follows immediately on the heels of his reference to the heavenly Son of Man. After saying, "What if you were to see the Son of Man ascending to where he was before?" (John 6:62) Jesus went on to declare, "It is the Spirit that gives life, the flesh is of no avail" (John 6:63). It is absolutely critical to interpret these two verses *together*, and not to isolate them from each other. When we do so, we immediately see that Jesus was not speaking about eating the dead flesh of his corpse (this would be cannibalism). Rather, he was speaking about eating the living flesh of his *resurrected body*, which would be raised to "life" by the power of "the Spirit" and then taken up to heaven in the ascension.

That is the other clue to the fact that new manna is miraculous: in the Eucharist, Jesus will give his crucified *and risen* body and blood. For, after his resurrection and ascension into heaven, his body would no longer be bound by space or time. He would be able to appear when he willed, and where he willed, and under whatever form he willed—just as he would later do on the Road to Emmaus (Luke 24:16, 31) or in the garden with Mary Magdalene (John 20:14). As the New Testament scholar Raymond Brown once put it, by referring to his bodily ascension, Jesus is saying "that it is not the dead body or flesh of Jesus which will be of benefit in the Eucharist, but his resurrected body full of the Spirit of Life."

Lest there be any doubt of this connection between the Eucharist and the bodily resurrection, go back to the bread of life sermon for a moment and notice the prominence of Jesus' reference to the resurrection:

> Amen, amen I say to you, unless you eat the flesh of the Son of Man and drink his blood, you have no life in you; he who eats my flesh and drinks my blood has eternal life, *and I will raise him up at the last day.* For my flesh is real food and my blood is real drink. (JOHN 6:53–54)

With these words, Jesus directly links eating his body and blood with the bodily resurrection of the believer on the last day. One reason this link is important is that Jesus' response to the disciples' objections is sometimes misinterpreted as changing everything he has just said about the Eucharist into a mere metaphor. This idea goes back at least as far as Ulrich Zwingli, one of the leaders of the Protestant Reformation, who took one verse—"the flesh is of no avail" (John 6:63)—entirely out of context and treated it as if it alone were proof that Jesus was only speaking symbolically.

But Zwingli can't be right. For one thing, when Jesus said that the words he had spoken were "Spirit and life" (John 6:63), he was not saying that he was speaking only symbolically. In Greek, the word *pneuma* ("spirit") does not mean "symbolic." In both the Old and New Testaments, the Spirit is *real*, more real than anything in the visible material world. Earlier in the same Gospel, when Jesus said, "God is spirit [*pneuma*]" (John 4:24), he certainly did not mean that God was merely symbolic!

Even more important, in his response to the disciples, Jesus said that "*the* flesh is of no avail" (John 6:63). He did *not* say "*my* flesh is of no avail." These are two very different statements. Nor could he have said the latter without flat out contradicting himself. If you read the preceding sermon carefully, you will find that Jesus has just finished saying six times in only seven verses that it was necessary to eat his flesh in order to have eternal life:

> The bread which I shall give for the life of the world is *my flesh*. (v. 51)
>
> Amen, Amen, I say to you, unless you eat *the flesh of the Son of Man* and drink his blood, you have no life in you. (v. 53)
>
> He who eats *my flesh* and drinks my blood has eternal life. (v. 54)
>
> For *my flesh* is real food, and my blood is real drink. (v. 55)
>
> He who eats *my flesh* and drinks my blood abides in me. (v. 56)
>
> He who eats *me* will live because of me. (v. 57)

In light of these verses, Jesus' response to the disciples cannot mean that his own flesh is of no avail. People who make this argument often don't stop and realize that it would make the flesh that he offered on the Cross—not to mention the flesh he assumed in the incarnation—useless as well. But that is absurd, especially in the Gospel which emphasizes that the Word "became flesh" for the sake of saving humanity (John 1:14). By speaking of "*the* flesh" (Greek *ho sarx*) and not "*my* flesh," Jesus is simply using a standard expression for "that which is natural or earthly," as well as those who see reality only from this perspective. Proof of this can be found just a few chapters later in John's Gospel, when Jesus says to the Pharisees, "You judge according to the flesh [Greek *ho sarx*]" (John 8:15).

In other words, just as the Pharisees rejected Jesus because they did not recognize his supernatural origin but instead judged him only according to his appearance, so, too, Jesus' disciples did not believe his Eucharistic teaching because they didn't understand the supernatural nature of the new manna from heaven. They judged it only by its appearances. They didn't understand that he wished to give them his resurrected body and blood, miraculously present under the veil of bread and wine.

As an aside, I should also point out that in drawing this connection between the new manna and the resurrection of the body, Jesus was not really saying anything entirely foreign to ancient Judaism itself. For example, in one ancient Jewish commentary on Genesis, Rabbi Joshua states, "He who serves God to his death will be satisfied with *the bread of the World to Come*" (*Genesis Rabbah* 82:8).

In ancient Jewish thought, "the World to Come" was another way of talking about the age of salvation. At this time, God would not only fulfill the promise to bring the Messiah; he would also restore creation itself, by raising the dead and transforming the visible universe into "a new heaven and a new earth" (see Isaiah 64–65). If Jesus saw the Eucharist as the Rabbinic "bread of the World to Come," then, again, he could not have seen it as ordinary bread. Rather, it was a foretaste and pledge of the new creation. This is of course exactly what Jesus said in the bread of life discourse: whoever eats the new manna of the Eucharist will be raised up "on the last day" (John 6:54).

Last but not least, only when we grasp this connection between the new manna from heaven and Jesus' risen body are we able to explain his startling command to drink his blood (John 6:53–56). How could Jesus say such a thing when the Old Testament explicitly forbade the Israelites to drink the blood of an animal? I suggest that the very reason God forbids drinking blood in the Old Covenant is the same reason Jesus commands his disciples to drink his blood: "For the life [Hebrew *nephesh*] of the flesh is in the blood" (Leviticus 17:11). Jesus would have known the Law of Moses, and he would have known that the power of his own resurrected "life"—indeed, his "soul"—was in his blood. Therefore, *if the disciples wished to share in the "life" of Jesus' bodily resurrection, then they had to partake of both his body and his blood.* If they wanted a share in the life of his bodily resurrection, then they had to receive his blood, given to them as drink: "Unless you eat the flesh of the Son of man and drink his blood *you have no life in you*; he who eats my flesh and drinks my blood has eternal life, and I will raise him up on the last day" (John 6:54).

5

—————— ⟫•⟪ ——————

THE BREAD OF THE PRESENCE

Now that we've looked at the Last Supper through the lenses of the Passover and the manna, more questions arise. If Jesus intended to inaugurate the new exodus through his death and resurrection, then *how did he think God would be worshiped once the new exodus had begun?* In particular, how would God be present to his people, as he had been in the past, in the Tabernacle of Moses?

Although many scholars agree that Jesus was looking forward to the new exodus, they have tended to ignore the question of what he thought worship would be like after it had begun. From an ancient Jewish perspective, however, this would have been a very important question. Would there be a new Tabernacle, as in the first exodus? If so, what kind of sacrifice would be offered in it? Would worship consist of animal sacrifices, such as those described in the Book of Leviticus? Or would it be focused on some other kind of offering? For example, in the second century A.D., Rabbi Menahem of Galilee taught that "In the World to Come all sacrifices will be annulled, but the thanksgiving sacrifice will never be annulled" (*Leviticus Rabbah* 9:7). This is a remarkable vision. We have a Jewish rabbi, not long after the time of Jesus, foreseeing a future age in which all of the many sacrifices described in the Torah would cease, and just one would remain: the "sacrifice of thanksgiving" (see Leviticus 7). That's what Rabbi Menahem expected; what did Jesus expect?

In this chapter, I will try to answer these questions by exploring our third key to understanding the Last Supper: the mysterious Bread of the Presence. Curiously, many modern readers have never even heard of this holy bread that was kept in the Jewish Tabernacle, much less explored how it might shed light on the Jewish roots of the Eucharist.

Perhaps this is because references to the Bread of the Presence are buried in some of the most difficult parts of the Old Testament, such as the detailed description of the Tabernacle (Exodus 25) or the priestly rules and regulations of the Levites (Leviticus 24). Or perhaps it is because older English Bibles tended to translate the Hebrew references to this bread with the rather obscure expression "Showbread" (or "Shewbread"). As we will see below, this has created some problems for properly understanding the significance of this bread.

Whatever the reason for its being little known, in this chapter I will try to show that the Old Testament Bread of the Presence is an extremely important piece of the Eucharistic puzzle. Indeed, an exploration of the Jewish context of the Gospels suggests that Jesus not only saw the

Last Supper as the new Passover and the new manna from heaven; he also saw it as the messianic fulfillment of the Bread of the Presence.

In order to see these links between the Last Supper and the Bread of the Presence, we will once again have to go back to the Old Testament and Jewish tradition and the practices and beliefs that surrounded this mysterious bread.

THE BREAD OF THE FACE

Despite most readers' unfamiliarity with the Bread of the Presence, it is actually mentioned many times in the Jewish Scriptures. For our purposes, it is the two most detailed descriptions that stand out. The first comes from the Book of Exodus, the second from the Book of Leviticus. We'll take a moment to look at each in its turn.

The Bread of the Face of God

The Bread of the Presence first appears in the Old Testament during the exodus from Egypt. As soon as God is finished giving the Ten Commandments to Israel and sealing the covenant with them with a heavenly banquet (Exodus 20–24), he immediately begins to give them instructions for how they are to worship him. All these instructions revolve around the central place of worship, "the tent of meeting," also known as the Tabernacle (Exodus 26).

The first thing we need to remember about the Tabernacle is that God commanded Moses to make three sacred objects to be kept inside of it:

1. The Ark of the Covenant;
2. The golden Lampstand, known as the Menorah;
3. The golden table of the Bread of the Presence.

Intriguingly, even before God describes the Tabernacle itself, he focuses Moses' attention on the three sacred objects that will be kept in the Holy Place, the inner sanctum. It's obvious that these three objects are especially important. In fact, the Bible says that Moses saw the pattern for making them in a vision that was "shown" to him on top of Mount Sinai (Exodus 25:9, 40). In other words, the Ark, the Lampstand, and the Bread of the Presence are patterned on *heavenly* realities.

The first of these, the famous Ark of the Covenant, was a golden box in which the Israelites would later place the tablets of the Ten Commandments, the manna, and Aaron's staff (Exodus 25:10–22). On top of the Ark was the "mercy seat," a large golden cover where two "cherubim of gold"—that is, statues of angels—were to be placed. (Notice here that God evidently does not consider these golden *statues* of angels to be a violation of the Ten Commandments. Despite what some readers of the Bible have thought, the God of Abraham, Isaac, and Jacob is apparently not antigold or antistatue!)

The second object, the golden Lampstand, is more commonly known by the Hebrew word *menorah* (Exodus 25:31–40). This candelabra had seven branches and was decorated like a tree or bush covered with flowers. The priests were to keep it burning continually, since it was the only source of light inside the Holy Place.

Finally, and most importantly for us, there was the golden table on which the Israelites placed the Bread of the Presence. Here are the details of its description:

> And you shall make a table of acacia wood . . . You
> shall overlay it with *pure gold*, and make a molding
> of gold around it. And you shall make its plates
> and dishes for incense, and *its flagons and bowls*
> *with which to pour libations*; of pure gold you shall
> make them. *And you shall set the Bread of the Presence*
> *on the table before me always.* (EXODUS 25:23–24,
> 29–30)

This passage contains three important clues to the
meaning of this strange bread.

First, upon careful examination, you'll notice that the
bread was not the only item on the golden table. Next
to it were "flagons and bowls" for pouring "libations"—
that is, sacrificial drink offerings of wine (compare Numbers 15:5–7; 28:7). So, when it comes to the Tabernacle
of Moses, we can rightly refer to it as the *bread and wine*
of the Presence. Intriguingly, as the Jewish scholar Menahem Haran argues, this wine was different from all other
wine offerings, since it was not poured out by the priests.
Instead, this wine seems to have been *drunk* in a sacred
meal of bread and wine.

Second, as I mentioned above, most older English translations, like the King James Version, speak about the Showbread. However, the actual Hebrew expression is *lehem*
ha panim, which in most modern English Bibles is "Bread
of the Presence." The question is, how exactly should we
translate this expression? And what does it mean?

On one hand, some scholars translate the Hebrew as
"Bread of Display" or "Bread of Offering." From this perspective, the Hebrew expression refers to the bread being
placed *before God's "presence,"* that is, in front of the Holy
of Holies, where the glory cloud of the divine presence

would descend above the Ark of the Covenant. The main problem with this interpretation is that it fails to communicate what the Hebrew says. It tells us what should be done to the bread, but does not actually translate the Hebrew word *panim.*

On the other hand, some scholars argue that the expression should be translated as literally as possible. They point out that the word commonly rendered as *presence* is actually the Hebrew word for *face* (*panim*). Therefore, the most literal translation of the Hebrew is *the Bread of the Face.* From this perspective the meaning of the expression is clear, but the implications are enormous: the Bread of the Presence is nothing less than the Bread of the Face *of God.* In this view, somehow, the bread itself is a visible sign of the face of God.

In support of this second interpretation, we should remember exactly when the Bread of the Presence was first given to the people of Israel. In the Book of Exodus, God commands Moses to build the golden table of the Bread of the Presence (Exodus 25) *immediately after* the heavenly banquet that he and the elders participated in on Mount Sinai (Exodus 24). The reason this proximity is significant is that the account of the heavenly meal emphasizes that when they ate and drank, they also saw God:

> Then Moses and Aaron, Nadab and Abihu, and seventy of the elders of Israel went up, and *they saw the God of Israel.* . . . And he did not lay his hand on the chief men of the people of Israel; *they beheld God,* and *ate and drank.* (EXODUS 24:9–11)

In a word, when we put the giving of the Bread of the Presence in its biblical context, it seems that the earthly

"Bread of the Face" was meant to be a kind of memorial of the heavenly banquet in which Moses and the elders "saw" the God of Israel while they "ate and drank." That is also why God commands Moses to construct the table for the Bread of the Presence (along with the Ark and the Menorah) according to the heavenly "pattern" that he was shown "on the mountain" (Exodus 25:9, 40). The earthly Tabernacle is a visible sign of the invisible heavenly place of God, and the earthly Bread of the Presence is a visible sign of the invisible heavenly face of God.

As one Old Testament scholar puts it, in the bread of the Tabernacle, it is God "himself" who acts as "the host who presents himself to his believers, giving divine strength, divine life."

The Bread of the "Everlasting Covenant"

But there is more. In addition to the brief description of the Bread of the Presence found in the Book of Exodus, there is also a more detailed account in Leviticus. In this book of laws for the Levitical priests, we learn that the bread and wine were signs not just of God's presence, but of the covenant. In other words, this bread represented the sacred bond between God and the twelve tribes of Israel:

> And you shall take fine flour, and bake *twelve cakes* of it; two tenths of an ephah shall be in each cake. And you shall set them in two rows, six in a row, upon the table of pure gold. And you shall put pure frankincense with each row, that it may go with the bread as a memorial portion to be offered by fire to the LORD. *Every Sabbath day Aaron shall set it in order before the LORD continually on behalf of*

the sons of Israel as an everlasting covenant. And it shall be for Aaron and his sons, and they shall eat it in a Holy Place, since it is for him a most holy portion out of the offerings by fire to the LORD, a perpetual due. (LEVITICUS 24:5-7)

Several things are worth noting here.

First and foremost, the Bread of the Presence is explicitly identified as the sign of the "everlasting covenant" between God and Israel. As we saw above, this covenant relationship had been established through the events that took place on Mount Sinai, when Moses and the elders of Israel offered sacrifice at the foot of Mount Sinai (Exodus 24:8-11). It seems that the Bread of the Presence—which, again, was patterned on the heavenly vision "shown" to Moses on top of Sinai (Exodus 25:9)—was meant to be a memorial and *sign* of the same "covenant" that had been sealed with Israel at Sinai. That's why there are twelve cakes of unleavened bread—one for each of the twelve tribes.

Second, according to Leviticus, the Bread of the Presence was a "perpetual" offering, to be continually present before the Lord in the Tabernacle. It was to be a perpetual sign of the fact that although the Israelites were no longer at Mount Sinai, God was still with them. Intriguingly, Leviticus also implies that as long as the Bread of the Presence was inside the Tabernacle, the flames of the Menorah were to be kept burning "continually" alongside it (Leviticus 24:1-4). (In modern times, Catholic churches maintain a similar practice with their own Tabernacles in the form of the sanctuary lamp, which always burns when the Eucharist is present.) Whenever the golden table was taken out of the Tabernacle, the Levitical priests were to cover it with a veil (Numbers 4:1-5).

Third—and this is important—the Bread of the Presence was not just a symbol; it was also a *sacrifice*. Although many readers of the Bible are familiar only with animal sacrifice, there were in fact two kinds of sacrifice in the Old Testament: (1) "bloody" sacrifice, involving the slaughter of bulls, goats, and sheep, and (2) "unbloody" sacrifice, which often consisted of bread and wine. The Bread of the Presence was a kind of unbloody sacrifice, known in Hebrew as the *minhah* (compare Leviticus 2). Lest there be any doubt about this, notice that incense was also kept on the golden table. In the Old Testament, incense always accompanies sacrifices in order to symbolize their rising to heaven. Moreover, the prophet Ezekiel actually refers to the golden table of the Bread of the Presence as an "altar" (Ezekiel 41:21–22). In other words, this bread was both a meal and a sacrifice. It was both a gift from God to his priests (in the form of a meal) and an offering of the priests to their God (in the form of a sacrifice).

Fourth and finally, the Bread of the Presence was not just any sacrifice. It was a "most holy" sacrifice, which Leviticus says was to be offered up "every Sabbath day" by Aaron the High Priest. This link between the Bread of the Presence and the Sabbath is important to stress, since modern readers sometimes tend to think of the Sabbath primarily as a day of rest, not necessarily as a day of sacrifice. To be sure, after the development of the synagogue in Jewish cities outside Jerusalem (probably in the third century B.C.), weekly Sabbath worship consisted primarily of attending the local synagogue to pray, to study the Torah, and to sing hymns of praise to God. However, according to the Bible, there was also a *cultic* aspect to Sabbath worship. In the Tabernacle (and, later, the Jerusalem

Temple), the Sabbath was distinctively marked by priestly sacrifices, both bloody and unbloody. Significantly, the unbloody sacrifice offered each week was nothing other than the Bread and wine of the Presence. It was only after the Romans destroyed the Temple in A.D. 70—that is, after the time of Jesus—that the offering of all sacrifices ceased. Before that tragic event, every week, Sabbath worship revolved around the offering of the fresh Bread of the Presence and of the eating of the bread by the priests in the Holy Place.

In sum, when we look at the pages of the Old Testament, it should be quite clear that the Bread of the Presence stood at the very center of Israelite worship. Alongside the famous Ark of the Covenant and the golden Menorah, it was one of the three most sacred objects in the Holy Place, the inner sanctum of the ancient Tabernacle. No one doubts how important the Sabbath was in ancient Israel; the Bread of the Presence was *the* Sabbath sacrifice, the "most holy" offering. Finally, it was both the sign of the "everlasting covenant" with Israel and the Bread of the Lord's perpetual presence in the Tabernacle—the "Bread of the Face" of Almighty God. Clearly, according to Jewish Scripture, the mysterious Bread of the Presence was no ordinary bread.

"BEHOLD, GOD'S LOVE FOR YOU"

When we turn to ancient Jewish tradition to see what it has to say about the Bread of the Presence, we find ourselves in very much the same situation as with Passover and the manna. Several remarkable traditions, not found in the

Bible, bear witness to a developing reverence for the mysterious, even miraculous, nature of this bread.

The Bread of the Presence and the Priest Melchizedek

Anyone familiar with the Book of Genesis or the letter to the Hebrews will have to admit that one of the most enigmatic people in the Bible is the man called Melchizedek. This shadowy figure, who is mentioned only twice in the entire Old Testament, first appears in the biblical account of Abraham's victory over the pagan kings in the promised land. After rescuing his nephew Lot from captivity, Abraham (here called Abram) is joined by Melchizedek, who is both priest and king, and who offers a very special sacrifice to God:

> After [Abram's] return from the defeat of Chedor-laomer and the kings who were with him . . . *Melchizedek King of Salem brought out bread and wine; he was priest of God Most High.* And he blessed him and said: "Blessed be Abram by God Most High, maker of heaven and earth; and blessed be God Most High, who has delivered your enemies into your hand!" And Abram gave him a tenth of everything. (GENESIS 14:17–20)

Who is this mysterious king? Why is he the first man to be called "priest" in the Bible (in Hebrew, *kohen*)? And why does he offer a sacrifice of "bread and wine" to God, rather than, say, a bull, or a goat, or a lamb?

Let's try to answer these questions as simply as possible. For one thing, in ancient Jewish tradition, Melchizedek was widely believed to be none other than Shem, the righteous firstborn son of Noah. According to these traditions, Shem was the birth name of Noah's son, while Melchizedek, meaning "king of righteousness," was his royal title. Moreover, as the first-century Jewish historian Josephus attests, it was also believed that the city of "Salem" over which Melchizedek was king was none other than Jeru-*salem*, which later became the city of David and the place of the Temple (compare Psalm 76:1–3).

In any case, what matters for us is that Melchizedek's sacrifice of bread and wine was connected by Jewish tradition with the Bread and wine of the Presence. In one ancient commentary on Genesis 14, we find the following:

> "And Melchizedek king of Salem brought forth bread and wine" [Gen 14:18]. . . . Rabbi Samuel ben Nahman said: *He instructed him in the laws of the priesthood, "bread" alluding to the Bread of the Presence, and "wine" to libations.* The Rabbis said: He revealed Torah to him, as it is written, "Come, eat of my bread, and drink of the wine I have mingled" [Prov 9:5]. (*GENESIS RABBAH* 43:6)

In this interpretation, Melchizedek is not only marked out as the first priest-king in Jerusalem. His offering of bread and wine is also explicitly identified as the Bread and wine of the Presence, which he, as a priest, taught Abraham how to offer. Thus, for some ancient Jews, the Bread and wine of the Presence was not merely one of the sacrifices instituted at the time of the exodus. Instead, its origins went back to the early generations of mankind. At that time, *all* men were priests, not according to the order of Levi—whose priestly order was instituted after Israel worshiped the Golden Calf (Exodus 32)—but according to the priestly "order of Melchizedek" (Psalm 110:4). And the sacrificial offering of this primordial priestly order was nothing other than bread and wine.

The Miraculous Bread of the Golden Table

In addition to traditions about biblical figures like Melchizedek, we also find a number of traditions about how the Bread of the Presence was offered in the Jewish Temple at the time of Jesus. For example, in the Mishnah, the rabbis tell us that the loaves of the Bread of the Presence had "horns" on their corners, consisting of small pieces of dough that were rounded upward like the horns of a bull (Mishnah, *Menahoth* 11:4). These horns made the bread look like the bronze altar of sacrifice that was in the outer court of the Temple, thereby supporting the Bible's description of the bread as both sign and sacrifice.

Moreover, we learn that certain rabbis believed that something special happened to the Bread of the Presence when it was offered by the priests as a sacrifice to God. *Before* the bread was brought into the Holy Place to be offered in sacrifice, it could be laid on a marble table. But *after* the bread had been consecrated to God by the priests, it had to be laid on a golden table:

> In the Porch at the entering in of the House [=the Temple] were two tables, the one of marble and the other of gold. *On the table of marble they laid the Bread of the Presence when it was brought in and on the table of gold they laid the Bread of the Presence when it*

> *was brought out,* since what is holy must be raised
> [in honor] and not brought down. And within was
> a table of gold whereon the Bread of the Presence
> lay continually. (MISHNAH, *MENAHOTH* 11:7)

This ritual clearly shows that, for the ancient Jewish rabbis, the Bread of the Presence was extremely sacred— but only after it had been offered as a sacrifice to God in the Holy Place. Before being offered in sacrifice, it was just ordinary bread, and could be set on an ordinary marble table. But once it had been offered in sacrifice, it was now "holy"—in Hebrew, *qadosh,* meaning "set apart" or "consecrated." As such, it had to be placed on a table of gold, just as all of the vessels and furniture in the Holy Place were made of gold (see Exodus 25).

One other tradition even goes so far as to suggest that the Bread of the Presence, after it had been consecrated, actually displayed *supernatural properties.* After the priests took the bread out of the Holy Place, they would lay it on the "table of gold," so that they might eat it among themselves (Mishnah, *Menahoth* 11:7). According to the Jewish Talmud, during the reign of one particularly holy High Priest, even a small piece of the Bread of the Presence could provide miraculous sustenance:

> [During the whole period that Simon the Righteous
> ministered as High Priest], a blessing was bestowed
> upon the *'omer,* the two breads, and the Bread of the
> Presence, so that every priest, who obtained a piece
> thereof as big as an olive, ate it and became satisfied
> with some eating thereof and even leaving some-
> thing over. (BABYLONIAN TALMUD, *YOMA* 39A)

Can anyone familiar with the Gospels fail to think here of the famous feeding of the five thousand? On that occasion, Jesus multiplied five loaves of bread, such that "all ate and were satisfied," and there was even some "left over" (Matthew 14:20). From an ancient Jewish perspective, the Bread of the Presence, like the manna before it, was no ordinary bread. It was believed by at least some rabbis to have been miraculous.

The Bread in the Temple

Perhaps the most striking tradition of all is the last one we will examine. It, too, has to do with the Bread of the Presence in the Temple at the time of Jesus.

In Jesus' day, it was customary for Jewish men living in the land of Israel to go up to Jerusalem and the Temple three times a year in order to keep the feasts of Passover, Pentecost, and Tabernacles. ("Pentecost" is the Greek name for the Jewish festival of Weeks, which took place seven weeks after the Sunday during Passover week.) This custom was rooted in the binding law of God, given to Moses: "Three times in the year shall all your males appear before the LORD God, the God of Israel" (Exodus 34:23; 23:17). According to both the Jerusalem Talmud and Babylonian Talmud, at each of these feasts, the priests in the Temple would do something remarkable. They would remove the Golden Table of the Bread of the Presence from within the Holy Place so that the Jewish pilgrims could see it. When they removed the holy bread, the priests would elevate it and say the following words:

> They [the priests] used to lift it [the Golden Table] up and exhibit the Bread of the Presence

on it to those who came up for the festivals, saying
to them, *"Behold, God's love for you!"* (BABYLONIAN
TALMUD, *MENAHOTH* 29A)

If this tradition weren't so well documented, it would
be almost unbelievable. For one thing, it seems to be an
unheard-of breach of Temple etiquette. Aside from the
priests, no one was allowed to enter the sanctuary and look
upon the sacred objects contained inside the Holy Place.
But during the pilgrim feasts, the Jewish people were
allowed to see *one* of the sacred objects hidden behind the
outer veil: the Bread of the Presence. Even more stunning
is the declaration of the priests while elevating this holy
bread. How could the Bread of the Presence be so closely
tied to the "love" of God? From an ancient Jewish perspective, what could these words mean?

Although we can only speculate, it seems safe to suggest that the Bread of the Presence was a sign of God's
love because it was a sign of the covenant. In the Old
Testament, the covenant between God and Israel is frequently described in terms of a "marriage" bond, *a covenant of love* between the divine Bridegroom (God) and
his earthly Bride (Israel) (see Ezekiel 16; Isaiah 54; Hosea
1–2). As we saw earlier, the Torah explicitly states that the
Bread of the Presence was not just the "most holy" sacrifice
of the Sabbath; it was also the sign of the "everlasting covenant" (Leviticus 24:7). As the visible sign of this everlasting covenant, the Bread of the Presence was also the visible
sign of the divine Bridegroom's love for his Bride. Perhaps
that is why the priests could say to the people when they
held up the bread, "Behold, God's love for you!"

To See the "Face" of the Lord

One last question remains. Why is it that the priests would bring out only the Bread of the Presence? Why not the golden Menorah, or even the Ark of the Covenant?

Again, while we cannot be certain, the reason may ultimately stem from the Old Testament. Recall that above I mentioned how the Book of Exodus commands that all Israelite men take part in the three feasts of Passover, Pentecost, and Tabernacles. As several recent scholars have pointed out, most English translations say that the men should "appear before God." But the literal Hebrew reads, "Three times a year shall all your males *see the face of the Lord*, the LORD God of Israel" (Exodus 34:23; 23:17). In this line, the Hebrew word for the "face" of God is *panim*, the same word used for the "Bread of the Presence" or "Bread of the Face" (Exodus 25:30). In other words, by showing the pilgrims the Bread of the *panim*, the priests in the Temple were fulfilling the Law that commanded that they "see the Face" of the Lord. As the Jewish scholar Israel Knohl writes:

> It seems to me that the sages departed from convention and permitted the display of the Temple furniture before the pilgrims so as to allow them to fulfill their obligation "to see the face." Or, to put it another way, the presentation of these holy items before the large assembly created the experience of a public theophany. The Israelites who had longed for the Temple courts and asked "when may I come to see the face of God," went up to the Temple at the pilgrimage feast and gazed upon the vessels of the Temple-service that were

> brought out of hiding. In this way their spiritual
> thirst was slaked and they fulfilled the command-
> ment of the Torah that "three times a year each
> male must see the face of the Sovereign, the
> LORD, the God of Israel" (EXODUS 34:23).

These words are right on target, although I would clarify
one point. It seems reasonable to conclude that for ancient
Jews, the Bread of the Presence was not the *actual* face of
God but an earthly sign of his face. The Old Testament is
quite clear that no one could see the unveiled face of God
and live (Exodus 33:20). However, it is also quite clear that
when Moses and the elders of Israel went up Mount Sinai,
they saw something divine. As the Torah states, they "beheld
God, and ate and drank" (Exodus 24:11).

However we interpret these words, one thing is clear: to
a first-century Jew like Jesus, who certainly kept the feasts
in Jerusalem and probably witnessed the elevation of the
golden table, the Bread of the Presence was no ordinary
bread! It was not just some ancient relic of bygone days,
sealed forever in the inner sanctuary. Instead, according
to ancient Jewish tradition, this holy bread was the primordial sacrifice of Melchizedek, the miraculous food of
the Holy Place, the Bread of the Face of Almighty God.
Last but not least, this holy bread was a living, visible sign
of God's love for his people, the way his earthly people
could catch a fleeting glimpse of the ultimate desire of
their hearts: to see the face of God and live, and to know
that he loved them.

Or, one should say, it should have been all these things.
Tragically, like the sacrifice of the Passover lamb in the
Temple, the weekly offering of the Bread of the Presence
came to a bitter end in A.D. 70, when the Roman armies

destroyed the Jerusalem Temple. From that day to this, the offering of the Bread of the Presence has ceased. To this day, you can travel to Rome and see the famous Arch of Titus, commissioned by the Emperor Domitian to memorialize the overthrow of Jerusalem. There, carved into the stone, are images of the Roman soldiers carrying off from the Temple both the golden Menorah and the golden table of the Bread of the Presence.

JESUS AND THE NEW BREAD OF THE PRESENCE

With these biblical backgrounds and Jewish traditions in mind, we can ask the question, did Jesus himself ever refer to the Bread of the Presence? And, if so, how might this mysterious bread and wine shed light on his actions at the Last Supper? If Jesus saw himself as inaugurating the new exodus, did he think there would be a new sanctuary? What did he think it would be like? Would the bread and wine of the Presence have a place in it?

On at least one occasion during his public ministry, Jesus did indeed refer to the Bread of the Presence. He did so in the midst of a debate over his disciples' act of plucking grain on the Sabbath, which was seen by some Pharisees as breaking the Sabbath rest. Even though the Old Testament itself has no explicit command against plucking grain on the Sabbath, the oral tradition of the Pharisees prohibited it. This prohibition led to the following incident:

> At that time Jesus went through the grainfields
> on the Sabbath; his disciples were hungry, and

they began to pluck heads of grain and to eat. But when the Pharisees saw it, they said to him, "Look, your disciples are doing what is not lawful to do on the Sabbath." He said to them, "Have you not read what David did, when he was hungry, and those who were with him: *how he entered the house of God and ate the Bread of the Presence,* which it was not lawful for him to eat nor for those who were with him, but only for the priests? Or have you not read how on the Sabbath the priests in the Temple profane the Sabbath, and are guiltless? I tell you, something greater than the Temple is here." (MATTHEW 12:1–6)

In order to understand what's going on in this (admittedly dense) exchange of arguments, it's important to highlight and explain the three ways in which Jesus justified the actions of his disciples.

King David and the Priestly Bread of the Presence

First, Jesus defended his disciples by appealing to a story of how King David and his followers once ate the Bread of the Presence in the Tabernacle of Moses, even though they were not Levitical priests.

This story can be found in the first Book of Samuel. Once, when David was on the run from King Saul, he came to the Tabernacle of Moses (which was at that time located in the town of Nob) and asked the priest there for food. And this is what happened:

Then came David to Nob to Ahimelech the priest. . . . "Now then what have you at hand? Give

me five loaves of bread, or whatever is here." And
the priest answered David, "I have no common
bread at hand, but there is holy bread; if only the
young men have kept themselves from women."
And David answered the priest, "Of a truth
women have been kept from us as always when I
go on an expedition; the vessels of the young men
are holy, even when it is a common journey; how
much more today will their vessels be holy?" *So the
priest gave him the holy bread; for there was no bread
there but the Bread of the Presence, which is removed
from before the LORD, to be replaced by hot bread on the
day it is taken away.* (1 SAMUEL 21:1, 3–6)

As any ancient Jew would have known, this is a peculiar
story. For the Torah makes it pretty clear that the Bread
of the Presence could only be eaten by "Aaron and his
sons," that is, by the Levitical priests (Leviticus 24:9). But
David and his men were not from the tribe of Levi. To the
contrary, David was descended from a different tribe—
the tribe of Judah. So how could David and his men eat the
priestly Bread of the Presence without breaking the Law?

For one thing, they happened to be in a state of sexual ritual purity. Although it is a little-known fact, the
regular practice of sexual abstinence was not something
that began with the New Testament. Already in the Old
Testament, Israelite men practiced a kind of temporary
"celibacy" on two occasions: (1) whenever they were on a
military expedition, or (2) whenever they served as priests
in the Sanctuary. That is why the priest Ahimelech makes
the rather strange statement "There is holy bread, if only
the young men have kept themselves from women." He
could give the Bread of the Presence to them only if they

were in the required state of priestly purity. Luckily for
David and his men, they happened to be in just such a
state, since they were prepared for doing battle.

Even more important, David himself had not only
been anointed king by the prophet Samuel (see 1 Samuel 16). According to the Bible, David was also a *priest.*
For whatever reason, even scholars frequently forget this.
But it is still true. That is why David could wear the "linen
ephod," a priestly garment, and offer priestly sacrifices at
the altar, "burnt offerings and peace offerings" (2 Samuel
6:14–17). That is also why the Bible says "David's sons were
priests" (2 Samuel 8:18). Like father, like sons. But—and
this is important—David was not just *any* kind of priest.
He was not a priest according to the order of Levi, which
had been instituted after the worship of the golden calf in
the Sinai desert (Exodus 32). David was a priest according to the order of Melchizedek, the ancient priest-king
of Salem. As David himself says in the Psalms to his royal
successor:

A Psalm of David

The LORD says to my Lord,
"Sit at my right hand, till I make your enemies your
    footstool."
The LORD sends forth from Zion your mighty scepter.
Rule in the midst of your foes.
The LORD has sworn and will not change his mind,
"You are a priest forever after the order of Melchizedek."
(PSALM 110:1–4)

As this Psalm makes crystal clear, King David and all
his successors were not merely kings; they were also priests

of the order of Melchizedek, the first man to be called "priest" in the Bible (Genesis 14:18). And as such, as long as David was in a state of purity, he could eat the Bread of the Presence. So what appears to be a case of lawbreaking on his part is in truth nothing of the sort.

With this in mind, let's go back to the Gospels. In Jesus' response to the Pharisees' criticism of his disciples, he is saying in effect, "I am like King David, and my disciples are like his followers, and we can act like priests, because David was a priest, according to the order of Melchizedek." And remember, what was it that Melchizedek offered to God? Bread and wine.

The Priests in the Temple and the Bread of the Presence

The second way Jesus defended his disciples was by appealing to the fact that the priests in the Temple work on the Sabbath yet do so without breaking the law: "Have you not read in the Law how on the Sabbath the priests in the Temple profane the Sabbath, and are guiltless?" (Matthew 12:5). When he spoke of "the Law," he was alluding to the priestly codes of conduct in the Book of Leviticus. In Leviticus, it expressly states that the priests in the Temple *did* work on the Sabbath, by preparing and offering the Bread of the Presence:

> And you shall take fine flour, and bake twelve cakes of it. . . . And you shall set them in two rows, upon the table of pure gold. . . . Every Sabbath day Aaron shall set it in order before the LORD continually on behalf of the sons of Israel as an everlasting covenant. (LEVITICUS 24:5–7, 8)

When you think about it, this is remarkable. While all of the Jewish laity were resting from work on the Sabbath—even from baking and cooking—the priests were in the Temple offering the Sabbath sacrifices, which included the Bread of the Presence. They were, in effect, "breaking" the Sabbath and doing so right in the Temple itself!

Nevertheless, as Jesus points out, even though, at first glance, the priests are "profaning" the Sabbath, they remain "guiltless." Why? An exception is made for them *because they are priests*, because they are in the Temple, and because they are offering the Bread of the Presence. Yet again, the message to the Pharisees is, "My disciples can 'work' on the Sabbath, because they have the same privileges and prerogatives as the priests in the Temple."

Something Greater Than the Temple

But how can Jesus draw such an analogy? How can he say this when the incident with the Pharisees took place not in the Temple but in a Galilean grain field?

This question leads us to his third and final point, which is perhaps the most important of all: Jesus justified his disciples' actions by identifying *himself* with the Temple. Notice that his final response to the Pharisees was not an appeal to Scripture but to his own authority, his own mysterious identity. Stunningly, in defense of himself and his disciples, he said to them: "*Something greater than the Temple is here*" (Matthew 12:8).

As the context makes clear, these words were a veiled reference to himself. Indeed, he has said things like this on other occasions: "Something greater than Solomon is here," and "Something greater than Jonah is here" (Matthew 12:41–42; Luke 11:31–32). But "something greater than the Temple"? It is almost impossible to overestimate just how staggering such a claim would have been to Jesus' original Jewish audience. As any of the Pharisees would have known, the Temple was nothing less than *the dwelling place of God's presence on earth.* That is what made it so special. That is what made it holy. That is what made it different from all other buildings. It was the dwelling place of God. As Jesus himself says elsewhere, "He who swears by the Temple, swears by it and by him who dwells in it" (Matthew 23:21).

But this begs a very important question. If, to an ancient Jew, the Temple was the dwelling place of God on earth, then what on earth—who on earth—could possibly be greater than it? Although we can try to avoid the obvious, the only adequate answer is God himself, present in person, "tabernacling" in the flesh. Once again, we brush up against the mystery of Jesus' divine identity. Who is he claiming to be? What is he claiming to be? In a word, Jesus is saying that *he himself is the true Temple.* He himself is where God dwells on earth. He is the very presence of God.

Should there be any doubt about the divine nature of Jesus' claims, notice that he quickly followed it up by also referring to himself as Son of Man as the "Lord of the Sabbath" (Matthew 12:8). Again, as I said earlier, and as any ancient Jew would have known, there was only one "Lord of the Sabbath"—the one who had made the Sabbath when he made the world (Genesis 1). In light of these two claims by Jesus, it is not surprising that the Gospels record no response from his Pharisaic opponents. They probably went away in stunned silence at what appeared to be blasphemy.

Once we understand these three lines of defense, Jesus' otherwise baffling responses to the Pharisees not only make sense, they are also very revealing. For they show us that Jesus saw himself as a new David, and thus as a Melchizedekian king and priest. They also show us that he identified his disciples as priestly followers who could work on the Sabbath, like the priests who offered the Bread of the Presence. Finally, they make absolutely clear that he saw himself—indeed, his own body—as the new Temple of God. And remember, it was in the Temple that the sacrificial Bread of the Presence was both offered and eaten.

The Bread and Wine of Jesus' Presence

In books about the Last Supper, scholars are often puzzled by a peculiar feature of the meal. If it was in fact a new Passover, then why didn't Jesus take the roasted flesh of the Passover lamb and identify *it* as his body? Why did he focus instead on the bread and wine? Moreover, why would he choose to identify the bread and wine so intimately with himself? Where could he have gotten the (admittedly strange) idea that bread and wine could somehow represent a *person*?

To be sure, one can see how the breaking of the bread and the pouring out of the wine could be visible signs of his imminent death. The broken bread symbolizes his broken body, and the outpoured wine symbolizes the shedding of his blood. But you have to admit that when you think of common symbols of a person's presence, bread and wine are not the first things that spring to mind. That is, unless you are a first-century Jew, and you are talking not just about the presence of a human being but about the presence of God.

However, as we have seen, the notion that bread and wine could be signs of the divine presence was something that would have been driven home at least three times a year, at the feasts of Passover, Pentecost, and Tabernacles. As we just learned, at each of these festivals, the golden table of the Bread of the Presence would be brought out for the pilgrims to see, and the priests would declare: "Behold, God's love for you!"

In light of everything we've seen so far in this chapter, I think the case can be made that from Jesus' perspective, the Last Supper was not merely a new Passover; it was also the new bread and wine of the Presence. Although most readers don't look at the Last Supper in terms of the bread and wine of the Presence, I invite you to look again:

> And he took bread, and when he had given thanks he broke it and gave it to them, saying, "This is *my body* which is given for you. Do this *in remembrance* of me." And likewise the cup after supper, saying, "This cup which is poured out for you is *the new covenant in my blood....* You are those who have continued with me in my trials; as my Father covenanted a kingdom for me, so do I covenant for you *that you may eat and drink at my table* in my kingdom, and sit on thrones judging the twelve tribes of Israel. (LUKE 22:19–20, 28–29)

Although often overlooked, there are a number of intriguing parallels between the bread and wine of the

Presence and the bread and wine of the Last Supper, as illustrated below:

Bread of the Presence	*The Last Supper*
1. Twelve Cakes for Twelve Tribes	1. Twelve Disciples for Twelve Tribes
2. Bread and wine of God's Presence	2. Bread and wine of Jesus' Presence
3. An "Everlasting Covenant" (*diatheke*)	3. A New "Covenant" (*diatheke*)
4. As a "Remembrance" (*anamnesis*)	4. In "Remembrance" (*anamnesis*) of Jesus
5. Offered by High Priest and eaten by Priests	5. Offered by Jesus and eaten by the disciples
6. Eaten at the Golden "Table" (*trapeza*) in the Jerusalem Temple (Exodus 25:23–30; Leviticus 24:5–9)	6. Jesus' "Table" (*trapeza*) in the Kingdom of the Father (Luke 22:19–20)

What are we to make of these parallels? Are they just coincidence? I don't think so. Instead, it seems to me, by means of his words and actions, Jesus was indicating that the Last Supper was not merely the institution of a new Passover. Nor was it only the giving of the new manna of the Messiah. It was also the institution of *the new Bread and wine of the Presence*, the bread of Jesus' own presence.

In short, when Jesus wanted to signify the everlasting covenant that he would establish between God and his people, he did not choose the flesh of the Passover lamb to do it. Rather, he drew their attention to the bread and wine of the Last Supper, which he identified as himself, as his own body and blood. After his passion, death, and Resurrection, it was through this bread and wine, the new Bread of the Presence, that he would be with his disciples. That is why he says to them, "Do this in remembrance of me." When he wanted to leave them with a perpetual sign of his love for them, he gave them bread and wine: "This is my body which is given for you" (Luke 22:19). "This is my blood of the covenant, which is poured out for many" (Mark 14:24). *Like the priests in the Temple before him, by means of the Last Supper, Jesus was saying to the disciples: "Behold, God's love for you."*

THE REAL PRESENCE

We can wrap up this chapter by returning to the question with which we began the book. How is it that Jesus, as a first-century Jew, could have ever uttered the words "This is my body" and "This is my blood"? And how is it that the first Christians came to believe that the Eucharist really was the body and blood of Christ?

When we look at this question through ancient Jewish eyes, we can find an answer. If Jesus and the early Jewish Christians saw the Last Supper as the institution of the new Bread of the Presence, then it follows that they did not see it as ordinary bread and wine. It was, rather, the sign and instrument of Jesus' *real* presence. Just as God had been really and truly present to his people in the Tabernacle of Moses and the Temple of Solomon, so now Jesus would be really and truly present to his disciples through the Eucharist. And just as the old Bread of the Presence had been the sign of God's "everlasting covenant," so now the Eucharist would become the perpetual sign of the new covenant, sealed in his blood. And just as the old Bread of the Presence was also the Bread of the Face of God, so now the Eucharist would be the Bread of the Face of Christ. Truly, in the Eucharist, the early Christians could say with Jesus, "Something greater than the Temple is here."

But how are we to understand such a mystery? How can Jesus truly be present under the appearances of bread and wine? How is this even possible?

For one thing, as we've already seen with both the manna and the Bread of the Presence, the mystery of Jesus' presence in the Eucharist is closely tied to the mystery of his divine identity. If Jesus was only an earthly Messiah, then one could easily call into question—indeed, one could easily call blasphemous—the idea that his blood would be the perpetual sign of the "new covenant." And if Jesus was only a great prophet, one could readily object to the idea that his body would become the new bread of God's presence. None of the prophets ever said anything like this.

However, if Jesus was *more* than a prophet, if he embodied "something greater than the Temple," yes, if he was the *divine* Son of God, then the new bread and wine of his new covenant were not just symbols. In a word, the new Bread of the Presence was miraculous. After all, it would take just that—a miracle—for bread and wine to be transformed into the body and blood of the Messiah.

Perhaps that is why Saint Cyril of Jerusalem—himself a native of the Holy Land and bishop of the church in Jerusalem in the fourth century A.D.—makes exactly this point. In one of the most ancient Christian writings that we have on the Eucharist, Cyril uses the ancient Bread of the Presence to explain the mystery of Jesus' real presence:

> In the Old Testament also there was the Bread of the Presence; but this, as it belonged to the Old Testament, has come to an end; but in the New Testament there is bread of heaven, and a cup of salvation, sanctifying soul and body. . . . Consider therefore the bread and the wine not as bare elements, for they are, according to the Lord's declaration, the body and blood of Christ; for even though sense suggests this to you, yet let faith establish you. Judge not the matter from the taste, but from faith be fully assured without misgiving, that body and blood of Christ have been vouchsafed to you. (SAINT CYRIL OF JERUSALEM, *MYSTAGOGICAL CATECHESIS* 4:5–6)

Again, for all this to be true, Jesus' action at the Last Supper would have to have been a *miracle*, and not just a sign or symbol. But, as Saint Cyril himself also points out, this isn't really a problem, given Jesus' record of performing miracles of supernatural transformation. As Cyril says: "Jesus once in Cana of Galilee turned the water into wine, akin to blood; is it incredible that He should have turned wine into blood?"

6

---- ❧ ❧ ----

THE FOURTH CUP AND THE
DEATH OF JESUS

Let's take a moment to recap our journey through Jewish Scripture and tradition up to this point. We've seen
how the Jewish people in Jesus' day were awaiting the new
exodus of the Messiah, and how Jesus signaled the fulfillment of those expectations. We've studied their hope for a
new Passover, and how at the Last Supper Jesus identified
himself as the true Passover lamb whose blood would be
poured out in sacrifice. We've encountered their longing
for the return of the miraculous manna, and how Jesus
promised to give it to them in the form of his own body.
Finally, we've seen their devotion to the Bread of the Presence, and how Jesus fulfilled this mysterious sign of God's
covenant love in his actions over the bread and wine.

As we bring our examination to a close, there is one

final but very important point to make. At the Last Supper, Jesus not only looked *back* to the Jewish history of salvation—the Passover of Egypt, the manna of Moses, and the bread of the Tabernacle. He also looked *forward* to his own passion and death. By doing so, he deliberately tied his actions over the bread and wine at the Last Supper to both the history of redemption and his own "exodus" that he was to accomplish in Jerusalem (Luke 9:31). This exodus, the new exodus, would somehow take place through what was about to happen to him in the holy city, when he went to his death on the cross.

In this chapter, we will explore this connection between the Last Supper and what Christians have come to refer to as the Paschal mystery—the mystery of Jesus' passion, death, and Resurrection from the dead. In order to do so, we'll need to bring our journey full circle by returning to the topic of the Passover. This is entirely appropriate, since the expression "Paschal" mystery actually comes from the Greek word *pascha* (Passover). Jesus' Paschal mystery is, quite literally, a Passover mystery.

In this chapter, we will not focus so much on the Passover sacrifice in the Jerusalem Temple as on the Passover meal that was eaten by the Jewish people after the sacrifice had been offered. As I hope to show, when the Last Supper is compared to the ancient Jewish Passover meal, we find something very strange. We find that, according to the Gospels, *Jesus did not finish the Last Supper.* At least, he did not finish it in the Upper Room.

Before I begin, however, I should issue a small caveat. What I am about to argue is somewhat more speculative than the previous chapters. Nevertheless, as I will try to show, the hypothesis that Jesus did not finish the Passover meal in the Upper Room will provide us with a plausible historical explanation for three otherwise puzzling facts in the Gospels: Jesus' vow at the Last Supper *not* to drink wine until the coming of the kingdom; his description in Gethsemane of his impending death as "drinking" a *cup*; and Jesus' unexpected act of *drinking wine* at the last moment before he dies on the cross. In order to see how these can be explained, we'll have to return to the topic of the Jewish Passover.

THE SHAPE OF THE JEWISH PASSOVER MEAL

In an earlier chapter, we spent a good bit of time studying the ancient Jewish Passover sacrifice, and how the lambs were killed in the Temple. But in Jesus' day there was much more to Passover than just the sacrifice. There was also the Passover *meal*, which had its own rules and regulations, its own steps and stages. Eventually, this well-regulated meal came to be known as the Passover Seder, from the Hebrew word for "order."

Although we have no evidence that the Passover meal was actually called a Seder in Jesus' own day, the oldest descriptions of it outside the Bible do in fact describe a well-ordered sequence of actions. The most detailed descriptions we have can be found in two sources: the Jewish Mishnah and the Jewish Tosefta. We have used the Mishnah quite a bit already; the Tosefta was a collection of Jewish traditions put together shortly after the Mishnah as a supplement to the traditions found in the Mishnah. (The Hebrew word for "addition, supplement" is *tosefet*.) By studying the striking parallels between these ancient Jewish traditions and the descriptions of the Last Supper found in the first-century Gospels, scholars have been able to produce a plausible reconstruction of the basic shape of the Passover meal at the time of Jesus.

As we work through these Jewish texts, keep in mind that, with a few key exceptions, this is (to the best of our knowledge) what Jesus and the disciples would have been doing in the Upper Room on the night before he died. As we will see, the differences between the Last Supper and an ordinary Passover meal will be just as significant as the similarities.

The Four Cups of Wine

According to the most ancient descriptions we have outside the Bible, the Jewish Passover meal seems to have been organized around four cups of wine, which were essential to any celebration. Both the Mishnah and the Tosefta agree on this point:

> On the eve of Passover, from about the time of the Evening Offering, a man must eat naught until nightfall. Even the poorest in Israel must not eat unless he sits down to table, and *they must not give them less than four cups of wine to drink.* (MISHNAH, *PESAHIM* 10:1)

> On the eve of Passover, from just before the afternoon daily whole offering, a person should not eat, until it gets dark. Even the poorest Israelite should not eat until he reclines at his table. And they should provide him with *no fewer than four cups of wine.* (TOSEFTA, *PISHA* 10:1)

Notice two things here. First, the consumption of the Passover lamb was to be preceded by several hours of fasting, from the time of the evening sacrifice (about 3 p.m.). This should ring a bell for Christians who fast for a period of time before receiving the Eucharist, a practice going back to the ancient Church. Second, the drinking of at least four cups of wine was considered mandatory. Even the poorest person in Israel, for whom wine may have proved hard to come by, could not celebrate the Passover without these four cups.

Why was the wine so important? The rabbis don't say. But one reason may be that the overall structure of the Passover meal seems to have revolved around the drinking of these four cups of wine. Let's take a moment to familiarize ourselves with each of these stages so that when we return to the Last Supper we can see how it does (and does not) fit with the ancient Jewish Passover meal described in rabbinic literature.

The 1st Cup: Introductory Rites

According to the rabbis, the Passover meal itself would begin in the evening, shortly before "nightfall." At this time, the father of the Jewish family would gather his household together at a large table. There they would all recline around the table, apparently symbolizing the freedom won for them by God in the exodus from Egypt.

Once this was done, the introductory rites (this is my language, not the rabbis') of the Passover meal proper would begin with the pouring and mixing of the first cup of wine. The "mixing" refers to the mingling of the cup of wine with a little water. This first cup was known as the cup of sanctification—in Hebrew, the *kiddush* cup. Once the first cup was poured and mixed, the father began the meal by saying a formal blessing over the cup of wine and the feast day. According to the Mishnah, the standard Jewish blessing over wine went something like this:

> "Blessed are you, O Lord our God, King of the universe, who creates the fruit of the vine" (SEE MISHNAH, *BERAKOTH* 6:1).

After this blessing was said, the food would be brought to the table and laid out before the father. It consisted of at least four key dishes: several cakes of unleavened bread, a dish of bitter herbs, a bowl of sauce known as *haroseth*, and the roasted Passover lamb. Intriguingly, the Mishnah refers to the last of these as "the body" (Hebrew *guph*) of the Passover lamb (*Pesahim* 10:3).

At this point, a kind of preliminary course (what we call appetizers) would begin. The father would take some of the bitter herbs, dip them in the haroseth sauce, and eat them. He probably did the same for others at the table. Once he finished this, the opening rites were ended, but the meal proper had not yet begun.

The 2nd Cup: The Proclamation of Scripture

At this time, the second cup of wine would be mixed, but not drunk. This cup was known as the cup of proclamation—in Hebrew, the *haggadah* cup. Why? At this point in the meal, the father would begin to "proclaim" what the Lord had done for Israel when he set them free from Egypt in the exodus. Thankfully, the rabbis describe this second stage of the meal in some detail:

> Then they mix him [the father] *the second cup.* And here the son asks his father . . . "*Why is this*

night different from other nights? For on other nights
we eat seasoned food once, but this night twice;
on other nights we eat leavened or unleavened
bread, but this night all is unleavened; on other
nights we eat flesh roast, stewed, or cooked, but
this night all is roast." And according to the
understanding of the son his father instructs him.
He begins with disgrace and ends with the glory;
and he expounds from "A wandering Aramean
was my father . . ." [Deut 26:5] until he finishes
the whole section. (MISHNAH, *PESAHIM* 10:4)

Notice that the son's questions are directly tied to the
drinking of the second cup of wine. Notice also that the
father would answer his question by quoting a specific
section of the Bible: the story of the exodus from Egypt
and the entry to the promised land (see Deuteronomy
26:5–11). In this way, we can already see that an important part of the Passover meal was the reading of Scripture and the act of looking back to the redemption won
in the exodus.

But this was not all the father did. He would also
explain the meaning of the parts of the Passover meal—
the lamb, the bread, and the bitter herbs. According to the
Mishnah, this had been required at least since the time of
Rabbi Gamaliel, who was a contemporary of Jesus:

Rabban Gamaliel used to say: Whosoever has not
said [the verses concerning] these three things at
Passover has not fulfilled his obligation. And these
are they: Passover, unleavened bread, and bitter herbs: "Passover"—because God passed over
the houses of our fathers in Egypt; "unleavened

bread"—because our fathers were ransomed from Egypt; "bitter herbs" because the Egyptians embittered the lives of our fathers in Egypt. In every generation a man must so regard himself as if he came forth himself out of Egypt, for it is written: "And you shall tell your son in that day, saying, 'It is because of that which the Lord did for me when I came out of Egypt.' (Exod 13:8) Therefore, we are bound to give thanks, to praise, to glorify, to honor, to exalt, to extol, and to bless him who wrought all these wonders for our fathers and for us. He brought us out from bondage to freedom, from sorrow to gladness, and from mourning to a feast-day, and from darkness to great light, and from slavery to redemption; so let us say before him the Hallelujah!" (MISHNAH, *PESAHIM* 10:5)

The act of explaining the meaning of the meal was arguably the heart of this part of the meal. For one thing, it fulfilled God's original command to keep the Passover as a day of "remembrance" (Exodus 12:14). In addition, it was the point at which the past significance of the exodus and its present meaning merged into one. No matter how many centuries had passed, by explaining the meaning of the meal, each person was somehow made capable of sharing in the redemption won in the exodus.

In response, all of the Passover participants were "bound to give thanks" for what God had done for them. To express a spirit of thanksgiving, at this point, they would sing Psalms 113–114, which praised the Lord for his goodness and thanked him for saving Israel from Egypt (Mishnah, *Pesahim* 10:6). These two psalms, along with Psalms 115–118, were known as the Hallel Psalms, psalms of "praise" (Hebrew *hallel*), which would be sung over the course of the entire meal.

The 3rd Cup: The Eating of the Meal

Next, a third cup of wine would be mixed. It would signal the beginning of the actual supper, when the Passover lamb and the unleavened bread would finally be eaten.

Unfortunately, it is fairly difficult to reconstruct exactly what took place at this point, because customs varied from place to place. However, it probably consisted of at least three basic steps. First, a blessing would have been said over the unleavened bread, before beginning the meal. The standard Jewish blessing went something like this:

> "Blessed are you, Lord God, who brings forth bread from the earth" (SEE MISHNAH, *BERAKOTH* 6:1).

Second, the meal probably began with the serving of an hors d'oeuvre, consisting of a small morsel of bread dipped in the bowl of sauce. This morsel is referred to in the Mishnah as a kind of appetizer. It may also have been the "morsel" that Judas dipped in the "dish" before leaving the Last Supper to betray Jesus (John 13:26–27). Third, after the appetizer, the main meal would have been eaten, consisting primarily of unleavened bread and the flesh of the Passover lamb.

Once the meal itself was finished, the father would say another blessing over the third cup of wine. The third cup was known as the cup of blessing—in Hebrew, the *berakah* cup. When this cup was drunk, the third stage of the Passover supper was complete.

The 4th Cup: Concluding Rites

The concluding rites of the Passover meal, like most liturgies, were more concise. They consisted of two main parts.

First, the remaining portion of the Hallel Psalms would be sung. These were Psalms 115–118, the last of which was known as the Great Hallel. Now, this might not mean much if you aren't very familiar with these psalms. But Jesus and his disciples would have known them quite well, since they would have sung them every year at Passover, both in the Temple when the lambs were being slain and in the course of the Passover meal. Now, given what was about to happen to Jesus, *imagine him singing these words* at the Last Supper:

> What shall I render to the LORD for all his
>   bounty to me?
> *I shall lift up the cup of salvation*
> *and call on the name of the LORD* . . .
> Precious in the sight of the LORD
> is the death of his holy ones.
> *O LORD, I am your servant*;
> *I am your servant, the son of your handmaid.*
> You have loosed my bonds;
> I will offer you *the sacrifice of thanksgiving,*
> and call on the name of the LORD.
>
> (PSALM 116:12–13, 15–17)

This is exactly what Jesus is doing at the Last Supper: he is offering to God the "sacrifice of thanksgiving," the new "thank offering" (*zebah todah*), what Greek-speaking Christians would call the "thanksgiving" (*eucharistia*).

Even more striking, given what he was about to suffer on the cross, imagine Jesus chanting (probably in

Hebrew) these words of the Great Hallel on the night he was betrayed:

> Out of my distress I called to the LORD;
> the LORD answered me and set me free . . .
> *I shall not die, but I shall live,*
> and recount the deeds of the LORD.
> The LORD has chastened me sorely,
> but he has not given me over to death.
> Open to me the gates of righteousness,
> that I may enter through them and give thanks
>   to the LORD.
> This is the gate of the LORD;
> the righteous shall enter through it.
> *I thank you that you have answered me*
> *and have become my salvation.*
> *The stone which the builders rejected*
> *has become the head of the corner.*
> This is the LORD's doing; it is marvelous in our eyes.
>
>   (PSALM 118:5, 17–22)

Once again—as we have seen over and over in this book—when the Gospel accounts are placed in context of Jewish Scripture and Jewish tradition, they suddenly spring to life, with new meanings and astounding connections. In this case, the words of the Hallel Psalms are almost a kind of "script" for the servant of God who would offer up a "sacrifice of thanksgiving" (Psalm 116:17). In the midst of singing these Jewish hymns, it would have been easy for Jesus to see his own fate as Messiah outlined in the words of the suffering servant of God described in the psalms.

After the singing of Psalm 118, the fourth cup of wine would be drunk. According to the Mishnah, it was forbidden to drink any wine "between the third and the fourth cups" (*Pesahim* 10:7). This fourth cup of wine was known as the cup of praise—in Hebrew, the *hallel* cup. When it was drunk, the Passover meal was complete.

DID JESUS FINISH THE LAST SUPPER?

With these Jewish traditions in mind, we can now turn back to the details of the Last Supper and compare them with what we've found in the rabbinic writings. When we do so, we find similarities and differences with an ordinary Passover, both of which are very revealing. On the one hand, the most detailed account of the Last Supper (in the Gospel of Luke) does in fact mention more than one cup of wine. This provides a strong parallel with the descriptions of multiple cups in the Mishnah and Tosefta. Likewise, the Gospels of Matthew and Mark both speak of Jesus and the disciples singing "a hymn" at the end of the meal. This seems to clearly reflect the Jewish tradition of singing the Great Hallel. On the other hand, when we look a bit more closely at the Gospel accounts, they also seem to suggest that Jesus didn't actually finish the Passover meal.

Let's take a few moments to look at the details.

How Many Cups at the Last Supper?

How many cups of wine were there at the Last Supper? Before I ever studied rabbinic tradition, the answer to this question was easy: one. However, the Gospel of Luke says otherwise. This difference is easy to miss (I missed it for years) if you aren't familiar with the traditional four cups of the ancient Jewish Passover. But look closely at Luke's account, and there you'll see it:

> And when the hour came, he sat at table, and the apostles with him. And he said to them, "*I have earnestly desired to eat this Passover with you* before I suffer; for I tell you that I shall not eat it until it is fulfilled in the kingdom of God." *And he took a cup*, and when he had given thanks he said, "Take this, and divide it among yourselves; for I tell you that from now on I shall not drink of the fruit of the vine until the kingdom of God comes." And he took bread, and when he had given thanks he broke it and gave it to them, saying, "This is my body which is given for you. Do this in remembrance of me." *And likewise the cup after supper*, saying, "This cup which is poured out for you is the new covenant in my blood." (LUKE 22:14–20)

There they are—two different cups: one over which he gives thanks, and the other which he identifies as the new covenant in his blood. But which of the four Passover cups are they?

Thankfully, Luke gives the clues we need to answer the question. He refers to the cup that Jesus identified with his own blood as "the cup *after* supper" (Luke 22:19). In the rabbinic descriptions of the Passover, this could only refer to the *third* cup, the "cup of blessing" (the *berakah*), which was drunk after the meal. We find confirmation for this suggestion in Paul's first letter to the Corinthians, written around A.D. 50. In this letter Paul actually refers to the Eucharistic cup of Jesus' blood using the rabbinic expression for the third cup:

> The *cup of blessing* which we bless, is it not a partici-
> pation in the blood of Christ? The bread which
> we break, is it not a participation in the body of
> Christ? (1 Corinthians 11:16)

Now, if it was indeed the third cup that Jesus identified
as his blood, then the other cup mentioned by Luke is in all
likelihood the *second* cup, the "cup of proclamation" (*haggadah*). In support of this suggestion, it's important to note
that after saying the blessing, Jesus does in fact explain the
meaning of the unleavened bread, just like a Jewish father
would do after drinking the second cup. But instead of
referring to the past exodus from Egypt and the "body" of
the Passover lamb, Jesus identifies the bread with his own
"body"—that is, with himself (Luke 22:19). In other words,
the Last Supper was a Jewish Passover meal. But it was no
ordinary Passover. It was the new Passover of the Messiah.

Jesus' Vow and the Fourth Cup

These are not the only parallels between the Last Supper
and the Jewish Passover. When we turn to the Gospels of
Matthew and Mark, they also contain similarities and differences with rabbinic tradition that are potentially revealing. Immediately after the words of institution, Jesus said
something and did something that would have baffled any
ancient Jew:

> And he took a cup, and when he had given
> thanks he gave it to them, saying, "Drink of it,
> all of you; for this is my blood of the covenant,
> which is poured out for many for the forgiveness
> of sins. I tell you *I shall not drink again of this fruit*

of the vine until that day when I drink it new with you in my Father's kingdom." And *when they had sung a hymn, they went out* to the Mount of Olives. (MATTHEW 26:27–30)

And he said to them "This is my blood of the covenant, which is poured out for many. Amen, I say to you, *I shall not drink again of the fruit of the vine* until that day when I drink it new in the kingdom of God." And *when they had sung a hymn, they went out* to the Mount of Olives. (MARK 14:24–26)

Did you catch it? In both accounts, two things are strange.

First, he vowed not to drink of "the fruit of the vine" until the coming of the kingdom of God. This is a big problem. As any first-century Jew would have known, at this point in the Passover meal (just after supper), there was still another cup of wine to be drunk (the fourth cup). But Jesus said he wouldn't drink again—at least, not until the kingdom came.

Second, like other ancient Jews, after drinking the third cup, Jesus and the disciples "sang a hymn" (Greek *hymnesantes*). As most commentators recognize, this is clearly a reference to the singing of Psalms 115–118, the final Hallel Psalms. But notice again what is missing. Although Jesus sang the hymn, neither Matthew nor Mark says that he drank the final cup of the Passover meal, the fourth cup of wine. Instead, they say only that he and the disciples "went out" of the Upper Room, out of Jerusalem, and across the valley to the Mount of Olives.

When we put these two things together—Jesus' vow not to drink wine again and the silence about him drinking the fourth cup—a compelling case can be made that Jesus both referred to the fourth Passover cup and refused to drink it at the Last Supper. This, at least, was the opinion of the great twentieth-century Jewish scholar David Daube, who years ago argued the following:

> There is . . . in Matthew and Mark a reference also to the fourth and last cup of the Passover liturgy. It is contained in the words: "I will not drink henceforth of this fruit of the vine until I drink it new in my father's kingdom" or "in the kingdom of God." *The meaning is that the fourth cup will not be taken, as would be the normal thing, at a subsequent stage of the service; it will be postponed till the kingdom is fully established* . . . [In this light,] the notice that "when they had sung a hymn they went out into the mount of Olives" now acquires a fuller sense. The implication is that they go out directly after the "hymn," without drinking the fourth cup and probably also without reciting "the blessing of the song." This portion of the liturgy is postponed till the arrival of the actual, final kingdom.

In other words, when the Last Supper is viewed through Jewish eyes, *Jesus did not actually finish his last Passover meal.* This is extremely significant. Jesus not only altered the meal by focusing on his own body and blood rather than the flesh of the paschal lamb. He also seems to have deliberately left the Passover liturgy incomplete, by vowing not to drink of the "fruit of the vine" and by leaving the Upper Room without doing so.

It is hard to overestimate just how puzzled the disciples must have been by such actions. (Although, by this point in

Jesus' ministry, they might have become fairly accustomed to being surprised.) Every other Jewish Passover they had ever attended would have ended with the celebratory drinking of the fourth cup, the *hallel* "cup of praise." But this Passover was cut short. This meal was different. Why? Why did Jesus vow not to drink of the Passover wine until the coming of the kingdom of God? Why did he leave the Upper Room after singing the hymn?

Jesus' Prayer in Gethsemane

The answer to this question may lie not in the Last Supper itself but in events surrounding Jesus' subsequent passion and death. Indeed, strong support for David Daube's interpretation of Jesus' vow can be found in the accounts of Jesus' agony in the garden of Gethsemane. Although many readers may be familiar with the scene, read it again, with the Last Supper and Passover liturgy in mind:

> Then Jesus went out with them to a place called Gethsemane, and he said to his disciples, "Sit here, while I go over there and pray." And taking with him Peter and the two sons of Zebedee, he began to be sorrowful and troubled. Then he said to them, "My soul is very sorrowful, even to death; remain here, and watch with me." And going a little farther he fell on his face and prayed, "*My Father, if it be possible, let this cup pass from me; nevertheless, not as I will, but as you will.*" And he came to the disciples and found them sleeping; and he said to Peter, "So, could you not watch with me one hour? Watch and pray that you may not enter into temptation; the spirit indeed is will-

ing, but the flesh is weak." Again for the second time, he went away and prayed, *"My Father, if this cannot pass unless I drink it, your will be done."* And again he came and found them sleeping, for their eyes were heavy. So, leaving them again, he went away and prayed for the third time, *saying the same words.* Then he came to the disciples and said to them, "Are you still sleeping and taking your rest? Behold, the hour is at hand, and the Son of man is betrayed into the hands of sinners. Rise, let us be going; see, my betrayer is at hand." (MATTHEW 26:36–46)

There it is, as plain as day. In the garden of Gethsemane, in the midst of his distress, Jesus prayed to the Father *three times* about the "cup" that he must drink. Why? Isn't this a rather strange way to refer to a crucifixion? Why did Jesus describe his death through the metaphor of drinking a cup? To what cup did he refer?

Given the Passover context of his prayer (it is still Passover night), and given the fact that he had just left the Upper Room, by now, the answer seems clear: Jesus is praying to the Father about the fourth cup, the final cup of the Passover liturgy. He has just celebrated the Last Supper, in which he identified his own *body* as the sacrifice of the new Passover. He has also just identified one of the cups of wine as his own *blood*, about to be poured out for the forgiveness of sins. In other words, Jesus implicitly identified himself as the new Passover lamb. The implication of this self-identification is sobering: *by the time this new Passover is finished, Jesus will be dead.* That's what happens to Passover lambs. They don't make it out alive.

In short, through his words of institution and his

prayer in Gethsemane, Jesus has woven his own fate into the completion of the Jewish Passover meal. When the meal is finished, and the final cup, drunk, it will mean his own death has arrived. That is why Jesus did not finish the Last Supper. That is why Jesus didn't drink the fourth cup. As the Protestant commentator William Lane states:

> The cup from which Jesus abstained was the fourth, which ordinarily concluded the Passover fellowship. . . . Jesus had used the third cup, associated with the promise of redemption, to refer to his atoning death on behalf of the elect community. The cup which he refused was the cup of consummation.

If this interpretation is correct—and I think it is—then there's really only one last question for us to ask, did Jesus *ever* finish the Last Supper? And if he did, when did he drink the fourth cup?

I Thirst

One thing is clear: Jesus did not drink the final cup of wine on the way to the cross.

After Judas arrived in the Garden of Gethsemane with the soldiers, a whole series of tragic events quickly unfolded. Jesus was arrested. He was brought before the Jewish council of chief priests and elders (known as the Sanhedrin), as well as before Pontius Pilate, the Roman procurator. He was publicly sentenced to execution, and then scourged, mocked, and handed over to be crucified.

But in the midst of all these sufferings, the Gospels make it a point to emphasize that Jesus did not drink of the fruit of the vine:

> And when they had mocked him, they stripped him of the robe, and put his own clothes on him, and led him away to crucify him. As they were marching out, they came upon a man of Cyrene, Simon by name; this man they compelled to carry his cross. And when they came to a place called Golgotha (which means "the place of the skull"), *they offered him wine to drink, mingled with gall; but when he tasted it, he would not drink it.* And when they had crucified him, they divided his garments among them by casting lots; then they sat down and kept watch over him there. (MATTHEW 27:31–36)

This is Matthew's account. Mark says the same thing, but even more forcefully: "They offered him wine mingled with myrrh; but *he did not take it*" (Mark 15:23). Why not?

The Jewish Custom of Giving Wine to the Dying

One possible explanation comes from the ancient Jewish custom of giving "wine" to a man sentenced to death. This custom is referred to in the Talmud:

> When one is led out to execution, he is given a goblet of wine containing a grain of frankincense, in order to benumb his senses, for it is written, "Give strong drink unto him that is ready to perish, and wine unto the bitter in soul" [Prov 31:6]. And it has

> also been taught: The noble women in Jerusalem
> used to donate and bring it.
>
> (BABYLONIAN TALMUD, *SANHEDRIN* 43A)

Two things are interesting about this tradition. First, it explains why Jesus was offered wine on the way to the cross: it was an act of mercy, done in order to numb his senses before experiencing the horrible pain of death by crucifixion. From this perspective, Jesus refused to drink the wine while carrying the cross because he did not wish to dull the pain of his sufferings in the midst of his passion. Second, this custom may also explain how Jesus could have deliberately left the Passover incomplete, while still expecting to eventually drink of the fruit of the vine. Even apart from any prophetic foreknowledge on his part, if he knew of the Jewish custom of giving wine to those condemned to die—which for the Talmud is rooted in a biblical command (Proverbs 31:6)—he could reasonably count on receiving the same mercy in the final moments of his life.

Either way, when we turn from the carrying of the cross to Jesus' final moments before he died, we find something surprising. We find that, at the very end, Jesus *did* in fact drink of "the fruit of the vine." Both Matthew and Mark say so, telling us that one of the bystanders "took a sponge, filled it with sour wine and put it on a reed, and gave it to him to drink" (Matthew 26:48; Mark 14:36). The most detailed description of Jesus' death, however, comes from the Gospel of John. According to John, Jesus not only accepted the wine of his execution; he explicitly *requested* a drink at the moment before his death:

> After this Jesus, knowing that all was now fin-
> ished, said (to fulfill the Scripture), "*I thirst.*" A

bowl full of sour wine stood there; so they put a
sponge full of the wine on hyssop and held it to
his mouth. *When Jesus had received the wine, he said,*
"It is finished"; and he bowed his head and gave up
his spirit. (JOHN 19:23–30)

Notice what just happened. When Jesus said, "It is finished," he was not just referring to his life or his messianic mission. For he did not say it until his request for
a drink had been answered. He did not say it until "he
had received the wine." Why? What does this mean? Once
again, when we remember Jesus' vow at the Last Supper,
and his prayer about drinking the "cup" in Gethsemane,
then the meaning of Jesus' last word becomes clear. It
means that Jesus did in fact drink the fourth cup of the
Jewish Passover. It means that he did in fact finish the Last
Supper. But he did not do it in the Upper Room. He did
it on the cross. He did it at the very moment of his death.

The New Sacrifice of the New Passover

If this interpretation is correct, then there are at least
three implications for how Jesus seems to have understood
his own death.

First, by vowing not to drink the final cup of the Last
Supper, Jesus *extended* his last Passover meal to include his
own suffering and death. In this way, the Last Supper was
not just a symbolic enactment of how he was going to die.
It was a prophetic sign that actually set his passion and
death in motion, a sign that was not totally complete until
his life had come to its end.

Second, by praying three times in Gethsemane for the "cup"
to be taken from him, Jesus *revealed* that he understood his own

death in terms of the Passover sacrifice. For, when the final cup of the meal was drunk, his own sacrifice would be complete, and his blood would be "poured out" like that of the Passover lambs. To be sure, the order of this new Passover is reversed. In the old Passover, the sacrifice of the lamb would come first, and then the eating of its flesh. But in this case, because Jesus had to institute the new Passover before his death, he preenacted it, as both host of the meal and sacrifice.

Third and finally, and most important of all, by waiting to drink the fourth cup of the Passover until the very moment of his death, Jesus *united* the Last Supper to his death on the cross. By refusing to drink of the fruit of the vine until he gave up his final breath, he joined the offering of himself under the form of bread and wine to the offering of himself on Calvary. Both actions said the same thing: "This is my body, given for you" (Luke 22:19). Both were done "for the forgiveness of sins" (Matthew 26:28). Both were done "as a ransom for many" (Mark 10:45). In short, *by means of the Last Supper, Jesus transformed the Cross into a Passover, and by means of the Cross, he transformed the Last Supper into a sacrifice.*

This link between the Last Supper and the Cross—between Holy Thursday and Good Friday—is worth pausing to consider. For most Christians, the idea that Jesus' death on the Cross was a "sacrifice" is a given, almost a commonplace. But this would not have been the case for any Jewish passerby who happened to witness the crucifixion. All he or she would have seen was one more torturous Roman *execution*—not a sacrifice. From an ancient Jewish perspective, in order to have a sacrifice, you need a *priest*, you need an *offering*, you need a *liturgy*. None of these were present at Calvary.

What was it, then, that made the early Christians refer to the crucifixion as a sacrifice? It was the Last Supper. For all of these things—a priest, a sacrificial offering of body and blood, a liturgy—were present at Jesus' final Passover meal. As the Protestant scholar A.E.J. Rawlinson says in his analysis of the Last Supper:

> Interpreting in advance the significance of his coming Passion, [Jesus] was in effect making it to be, for all time, what it otherwise would not have been, viz., a sacrifice for the sins of the world. *It is the Last Supper which makes Calvary sacrificial.* It was not the death upon Calvary per se, but the death upon Calvary as the Last Supper interprets it and gives the clue to its meaning which constitutes our Lord's Sacrifice.

This is one of the great "secrets" of the Last Supper, a secret that can only be unlocked by a close study of the Passover. When we view the supper and the cross through the lens of Jewish liturgy, it becomes clear that Jesus *himself* saw both events as one single sacrifice. That is why he united the offering of his body and blood in the Upper Room to the offering of his body and blood on the wood of the cross. That is why he instituted a new Passover liturgy that was directly tied to his death.

In sum, by refusing to drink the final Passover cup until his dying moments, Jesus gathered up everything that would happen to him between Holy Thursday and Good Friday—his betrayal, his supper, his agony, his passion, his death—and united it to the new Passover that would be celebrated "in memory" of him. As the memorial of his new Passover, the Eucharist therefore not only makes present the actions of Jesus of the Upper Room; it also makes present the sacrifice of Jesus on Calvary.

—————————— ❯❯ ❮❮ ——————————

7

THE JEWISH ROOTS OF THE
CHRISTIAN FAITH

Over the course of the last several years, I've spent a good deal of my time traveling around the country and speaking on the topics covered in this book. After the lectures are over, people who come up to talk with me have all kinds of different responses. A few, I'm humbled to say, have been moved to tears, for they see in the Jewish roots of the Eucharist a sign of the fact that God's hand is indeed at work in history, paving the way and preparing for what he would accomplish through the new exodus of the Messiah, who has indeed come. Others have found the faith of their youth strengthened and deepened, so that they are inspired once again to make the Eucharist the center of their lives. Still others have been challenged by a vision of the Eucharistic mystery that goes far beyond the symbolic meal celebrated on occasion in their various Christian denominations.

But there is one particular response, one particular question, that I almost always get. Over and over again, people come up to me and ask; "*Why haven't I heard this before?* Why haven't I heard more about the Passover, the manna, and the Bread of the Presence? Is all this some kind of biblical breakthrough?"

The answer may surprise you. Pretty much everything I've said so far—at least, everything worthwhile—has more or less been said before. Most of the ideas in this book are not new. In fact, they're quite old. And not only are they old, but they're fairly accessible. They can be found in the writings of the New Testament, the works of the ancient Christian writers known as the early Church Fathers (first through seventh centuries A.D.), and even in the official teachings of the Catholic Church.

In other words, one of the tasks of a theologian is to be a good thief—that is, to "steal" from the boundless treasures of Jewish and Christian tradition and use these riches to shed light on the meaning of the Scriptures. So, in this final chapter, I'd like to take a few moments to sum up what we've learned about Jesus and the Jewish roots of the Eucharist and show how these connections between the Old and New Testaments are not exegetical novelties, but part of the inherited tradition of the Christian faith.

Pascha Means Passover

As I have argued throughout this book, Jesus saw the Last Supper as a new Passover. From his perspective, therefore, it was no ordinary meal. It wasn't even an ordinary Passover meal. Jesus knew, like other ancient Jews, that the Scriptures foretold that God would one day save his people again in a new exodus. And he probably knew the rabbinic tradition that the Messiah would come on Passover night. He almost certainly believed that in order for there to be a new exodus, there needed to be a new Passover. And that's exactly what he set out to accomplish at the last Supper.

Therefore, Jesus not only celebrated the Jewish Passover that night in the Upper Room. As the long-awaited Messiah of Israel, the suffering servant who would give his life for "many" (Isaiah 53:10–12), Jesus also reconfigured the Passover around his own passion. By refusing to drink the fourth cup until his death on the Cross, he united the Last Supper to his own sacrificial death. And by commanding his disciples to repeat what he had done in the Upper Room, he deliberately perpetuated this new Passover—both sacrifice and meal—down through the ages. By means of these actions, he set the new exodus in motion. What mattered now was not the flesh of the Passover lamb that had been slain in Egypt, but his own flesh and blood that would be sacrificed on the cross. Jesus acted as the host of the messianic Passover, because he saw himself as the Messiah. He offered himself as a sacrifice, because he saw himself as the Passover lamb.

Over the course of his lifetime, Jesus had probably seen dozens of Jews executed on crosses at the hands of the Romans. He knew what kind of death awaited those who got into trouble with the Jerusalem authorities. And he had probably seen thousands of Passover lambs being carried on wooden crosses out of the Temple in Jerusalem to be eaten each spring. What made this Passover different was not that a lamb was sacrificed. That happened every year. What made this Passover different was not even that somebody got executed. That had happened before. What made this Passover different was that Jesus identified *himself* as the "unblemished male lamb" whose life would be given to deliver others from death (Exodus 12:1–6). He identified himself as the lamb of God whose "flesh" must be both offered *and eaten* "for the life of the world" (John 6:51).

In the end, Jesus' identification of himself as the new Passover lamb is the only historically plausible explanation for what he said to his disciples in the Upper Room. For he knew full well—just like other ancient Jews—that the Passover sacrifice was not completed by the death of the lamb. It was completed by a sacred meal. You had to *eat* the lamb. And not just a symbol of the lamb—but its actual flesh. Ultimately, that is the only way Jesus the Jew could have ever said to his Twelve disciples: "Take, eat; this is my body" (Matthew 26:26).

The New Passover in Ancient Christianity

Jesus' understanding of the Last Supper as a new Passover is also the best explanation for why the earliest Christian writers—both inside and outside the New Testament—would also speak of the Eucharist in terms of the Passover. Historically, this idea was rooted in the Jewish hope for a messianic Passover and in the actions of Jesus himself. However, the early Christians took it and gave it a central place in their explanations of the meaning and mystery of the Eucharist.

In the New Testament, there are a couple of key examples of this. In the last book of the Bible—the Book of Revelation—John the seer has a vision of Jesus in heaven.

What John sees, however, is not a man but "*a Lamb*, standing as though slain" (Revelation 5:6). The symbolism of this vision is powerful: the mystery of Jesus' identity is revealed in the heavenly Passover lamb, who is both crucified ("slain") and risen ("standing"). Through the power of this Lamb's "blood," believers are made into "a kingdom and priests to our God," just as the Israelites were called to be "a kingdom of priests" at the time of the exodus (Revelation 5:10; Exodus 19:6). This strongly suggests that the heavenly worship surrounding this Lamb—which John describes in great detail (Revelation 4–5)—is not just any liturgical celebration, but a heavenly Passover.

Equally striking, Saint Paul links the sacrifice of Christ as Passover lamb to the celebration of a new "feast" of unleavened bread among the Christians:

> Do you not know that a little leaven leavens the whole lump? Cleanse out the old leaven that you may be a new lump, as you really are unleavened. For Christ, our passover lamb, has been sacrificed. Let us, therefore, keep the feast, not with the old leaven, the leaven of malice and evil, but with the unleavened bread of sincerity and truth.
> (1 CORINTHIANS 5:7–8)

Remember that the Jewish Passover could only be celebrated with *unleavened* bread. In light of this, Paul is drawing out the moral implications of Jesus' identity as the new Passover Lamb. If Jesus is the new Passover Lamb, then Christians need to prepare to keep the new Passover "feast," the feast of the Eucharist. They do this not by cleaning out the leaven of the old Passover rite, but by cleansing their hearts of what that leaven symbolized:

the uncleanness of sin. Just as the Jews were to remove all leaven and to fast before receiving the Passover (Mishnah, *Pesahim* 10:1), so, too, Paul calls his Christian audience to cleanse their hearts before receiving the Eucharist, lest they "profane the body and blood" of Christ their Passover and thereby "eat and drink judgment" against themselves (1 Corinthians 11:27–28).

Outside the New Testament, we find the early Church Fathers saying similar things about the Passover. Saint Justin Martyr was a Greek philosopher who converted to Christianity in the second century A.D. In his famous dialogue with Trypho, Justin declares: "*The mystery of the lamb*, then, which God ordered you to sacrifice as the Passover, *was truly a type of Christ*, with whose blood the believers, in proportion to the strength of their faith, anoint their homes, that is, themselves" (*Dialogue with Trypho*, 40:1–3). Origen, arguably the greatest biblical commentator of his day, lived in the Egyptian city of Alexandria in the late second and early third centuries. In his writings, he speaks of the celebration of a new paschal feast:

> Some object that we, too, have the custom of observing certain days—for example, the Lord's day, the Preparation, the Passover, and Pentecost. . . . [However,] *he who considers that "Christ, our paschal lamb, has been sacrificed" (1 Cor 5:7) knows that it is his duty to keep the feast by eating the flesh of the Word,* and so he never ceases to keep the paschal feast. For *pascha* means Passover, and he is ever striving in all his thoughts, words and deeds, to pass over from the things of this life to God. He is hastening toward the city of God. (ORIGEN, *AGAINST CELSUS*, 8:22)

With the words "*pascha* means Passover," Origen gets right to the heart of the mystery of the Christian Eucharist. Because of God's commands, every Christian has the "duty" of "keeping the feast" of Passover. But how do they do this? Not by eating the flesh of the lamb, but by "eating the flesh of the Word"—that is, the flesh of the divine Word who became incarnate (John 1:14). Through the new Passover feast of the Eucharist, the Christian "passes over" from the things of this world to the things of God.

Thus, like the Jews at the time of the Temple, Christians are pilgrims journeying toward Jerusalem. However, in the case of the new Passover, the destination is no longer the earthly city of the earthly land, but the new Jerusalem of the heavenly city of God.

The New Passover Today

The story does not end, however, with the writings of the Church Fathers. The mysterious connection between the Jewish Passover and the Christian Eucharist is not an insight that is confined to ancient Christian tomes that nobody reads anymore. To the contrary, it is a vital part of the *living* teaching of the present-day Catholic Church, which draws its doctrines directly from Christian Scripture and apostolic Tradition.

These teachings are gathered together in a remarkable way in the official compendium of Catholic doctrine known as the *Catechism of the Catholic Church*, published and promulgated in 1992 by Pope John Paul II (hereafter cited as CCC). This precious jewel of a book is an overview of the entire Christian faith, one filled with insights from the Bible and the early Church Fathers. Throughout the book, the Church repeatedly uses the biblical and Jewish roots of the Christian faith to illuminate the mystery of the Eucharist.

For example, when it turns to the topic of the Eucharist, the Catechism teaches that at the Last Supper, Jesus not only fulfilled the ancient Jewish Passover. He also anticipated the new Passover that he would accomplish in his passion and death:

> Jesus chose the time of Passover to fulfill what he had announced at Capernaum; giving his disciples his Body and Blood. . . . *By celebrating the Last Supper with his apostles in the course of the Passover meal, Jesus gave the Jewish Passover its definitive meaning.* Jesus' passing over to his father by his death and Resurrection, *the new Passover,* is anticipated in the Supper and celebrated in the Eucharist, which fulfills the Jewish Passover and anticipates the final Passover of the Church in the glory of the kingdom. (CCC 1339–1340)

There it is, plain and simple. What took me years of study to figure out, the Church declares with enviable brevity: Jesus' death, resurrection, and ascension are nothing less than a "new Passover." Through the Last Supper, Jesus makes the disciples "sharers in his Passover" (CCC 1337). Moreover, because "the Eucharist is the memorial of Christ's Passover" (CCC 1362), it not only commemorates Jesus' death and Resurrection; it actually makes that event a present reality. "When the Church celebrates the Eucharist, she commemorates Christ's Passover, and it is made present: the sacrifice Christ offered once for all on the cross remains ever present" (CCC 1364).

Fascinatingly, the Catechism even recognizes the

connections between the third cup of the Jewish Passover, the cup of the Last Supper, the cup of Gethsemane, and the "cup" drunk by Jesus on the cross:

> The "cup of blessing" at the end of the Jewish Passover meal adds to the festive joy of wine an eschatological dimension: the messianic expectation of the rebuilding of Jerusalem. When Jesus instituted the Eucharist, he gave a new and definitive meaning to the blessing of the bread and the cup. (ccc 1334)

> The cup of the New Covenant, which Jesus anticipated when he offered himself at the Last Supper, is afterwards accepted by him from his Father's hands in his agony in the garden of Gethsemani, making himself "obedient unto death." Jesus prays: "My Father, if it be possible, let this cup pass from me . . ." (ccc 612)

> The desire to embrace his Father's plan of redeeming love inspired Jesus' whole life, for his redemptive passion was the very reason for his Incarnation. And so he asked . . . "Shall I not drink the cup which the Father has given me." From the cross, just before "It is finished," he said, "I thirst." (ccc 608)

To be sure, in these passages, the Catechism does not go so far as to identify the wine drunk by Jesus on the Cross as the fourth cup of the Jewish Passover. Nevertheless, it does see in Jesus' final words the completion of his act of drinking "the cup" of redemption that he had prayed about in Gethsemane and "anticipated" in the Last Supper.

Years ago, before I began working on this book, I have to confess that I never really thought of the Last Supper as a new Passover. I don't know *why* I never thought of it that way; I just didn't. I knew that Jesus celebrated the Last Supper during Passover, and I knew that, in a certain sense, this was the first "Eucharist." But I didn't put two and two together. I never connected the dots. What I can say now is that my own ignorance did not stem from the idea being lost in the passing sands of time. To the contrary, the New Testament, the Church Fathers, and the contemporary teaching of the Catholic Church make it abundantly clear. The Last Supper—and, by extension, the Christian Eucharist—are nothing less than the new Passover of Christ, the new Passover of the Messiah.

THE SHADOW OF THE MANNA

As we learned in Chapter 4, "The Manna of the Messiah," Jesus spoke of the gift he would give at the Last Supper as new manna from heaven. In a certain sense, the manna is even more important than the Passover. If we truly want to unravel the mystery of the Last Supper, we've got to understand that Jesus not only saw the Eucharist as a very special Passover meal. He saw it as a *miracle*. He saw it as supernatural.

As a first-century Jew, Jesus knew well that in the Old Testament, the manna was no ordinary bread. It was miraculous "bread from heaven" (Exodus 16:4). The manna had begun with a miracle, when God rained "bread" and "flesh" from heaven during the exodus. The manna also ended with a miracle, when it mysteriously stopped, immediately after the Israelites reached the promised land. In other words, like any other ancient Jew, Jesus would have known that the Bible taught that the manna was a heavenly reality. It was not ordinary food; it was the "bread of angels" (Psalm 78:25).

And if Jesus was familiar with ancient Jewish tradition, then he would have known still more. He would have known that some Jews believed that the manna had existed in heaven since the very beginning of the world. He would have known that others believed that the manna still existed in the heavenly Temple. And he certainly knew— because his fellow Jews reminded him of it when he taught at Capernaum—that when the Messiah finally came, he would bring down "the treasury of manna" once again (*2 Baruch* 29:8). The manna of Moses would be transcended by the manna of the Messiah.

If Jesus knew all this, then when he deliberately chose to identify the Eucharist with the new manna from heaven, he thereby revealed that he, too, saw it as miraculous. The Eucharist would be the "supernatural bread" of the new exodus that he taught his disciples to pray for every day (Matthew 6:13; Luke 11:3). Unlike the old manna, which only communicated natural life, this new manna would give supernatural life: "he who eats this bread will live for ever" (John 6:58). The old manna had been a miraculous foretaste of the promised land. The new manna of the Eucharist would be a miraculous foretaste of the bodily resurrection. That is why Jesus told the disciples it was necessary for them to eat it in order to be "raised up" on the last day. If they wanted to receive the "life" of the bodily resurrection, they had to eat the miraculous food of the resurrection. If they wanted to enter the new promised land of the new creation (what the rabbis called the World to Come), they had to eat the food of the new creation (what the rabbis called the "bread of the world to come," *Genesis Rabbah* 82:8). And the world to come was no mere symbol; it was real.

Should there be any doubt about this, it's important to remember that Jesus had performed miracles before. During his public ministry, that's what he spent a good bit of his time doing. He healed the sick. He raised the dead. And, if you recall from Chapter 4, on one occasion, he even fed five thousand people in the desert with miraculous bread. According to the Gospel of John, this took place almost a year before Jesus' passion and death, during the spring, near the time of the feast of Passover (John 6:4). Significantly, the feeding of the five thousand in the wilderness not only looked back to the manna of Moses. It also anticipated what Jesus was going to do at the Last Supper. Compare the two events in the Gospels:

The Feeding of the Five Thousand	*The Last Supper*
1. Took place in the evening	1. Took place in the evening
2. The people were "reclining"	2. Jesus and the disciples were "reclining"
3. Jesus took five loaves	3. Jesus took bread
4. Jesus blessed	4. Jesus blessed
5. Jesus broke the bread	5. Jesus broke the bread
6. Jesus "gave thanks" (*eucharistesas*)	6. Jesus "gave thanks" (*eucharistesas*)
7. Jesus gave it to the disciples	7. Jesus gave it to the disciples
(Mark 6:35–44; John 6:11)	(Mark 14:17–25)

Is one of these a miracle, and one just a symbolic action? Or are they *both* miracles—one pointing forward to the other? I would suggest the latter. I would suggest that the miraculous "thanksgiving" (*eucharistia*) of the feeding of the five thousand (John 6:11) pointed toward the miraculous "thanksgiving" (*eucharistia*) of the Last Supper (Mark 14:23). And the Gospel writers knew it. That's why they emphasized the parallels between the two. At the feeding of the five thousand, Jesus performed a sign that the new manna was coming. At the Last Supper, it came.

In short, there was above all one reason why Jesus the Jew could identify the Eucharist as the new manna from heaven. In his eyes, the Last Supper was not just a Passover sacrifice; it was a miracle of the new and greater exodus. At that final supper, Jesus miraculously transformed bread and wine into his own body and blood. In doing so, he gave the disciples a share in both his bodily death and his bodily resurrection. In doing so, he gave the disciples the "supernatural bread" that would sustain them each day on their journey toward the new promised land of the new creation, a foretaste of the reality of the life of the world to come.

The New Manna in Ancient Christianity

Once again, when we turn to the writings of the New Testament and the early Church Fathers, we find that they, too, saw the Eucharist as the fulfillment of the ancient miracle of the manna from heaven.

Intriguingly, for a second time, our two New Testament witnesses are the Apostle Paul and the Book of Revelation. At the beginning of John's Apocalypse, the Spirit of God tells him to encourage one of his churches with the following words: "He who has an ear, let him hear what the Spirit says to the churches. To him who conquers I will give some of the hidden manna" (Revelation 2:17). Although commentators continue to debate exactly what this refers to, some see in it a reference to the Eucharist, in which John is drawing on the Old Testament manna that was "hidden" in the Tabernacle (Exodus 16:32–36).

No such ambiguity exists in Paul's first letter to the Corinthians. In this letter, he begins a long discussion of the Christian Eucharist (chapters 11–12) by going back to the miracle of the manna in the desert:

> I want you to know, brethren, that our fathers
> were all under the cloud, and all passed through
> the sea, and all were baptized into Moses in the
> cloud and in the sea, and *all ate the same supernat-*
> *ural food and all drank the same supernatural drink.*
> (1 CORINTHIANS 10:1–2)

Paul's message to the Corinthians is clear: don't act like the wilderness generation of the exodus, many of whom died because they despised the manna as "worthless food" and they began to practice idolatry (1 Corinthians 10:6–13; see Numbers 21:4–9). To the contrary, Christians need to recognize and respect the supernatural food and drink they have been given in the Eucharist. That is why Paul moves straight from his discussion of the manna to his Eucharistic exhortation: "The cup of blessing which we bless, is it not a communion in the blood of Christ? The bread which we break, is it not a communion in the body of Christ?" (1 Corinthians 10:16). The new supernatural food of the new exodus is the new manna of the body of Christ.

None of these connections were lost on the ancient Christian writers, who used these very passages from the New Testament—in addition to Jesus' sermon in Capernaum (John 6)—to show that Christ, present in the Eucharist, is the new manna from heaven. For example, Origen says of Israel's journey in the desert: "Then, in likeness, manna was food. Now, in reality, the flesh of the Word of God is true food. As he himself says, 'My flesh is food indeed, and my blood is drink indeed'" (*On Numbers* 7:2).

Even more explicit are the comments of Tyconius (ca. A.D. 330–390), a lay theologian and biblical interpreter in North Africa, who writes in his commentary on the Book of Revelation:

> "To him who conquers I will give some of the hidden manna" (Rev 2:17). This manna is the invisible Bread which came down from heaven, which indeed was made man, so that "man might eat the bread of angels" (Psa 78:25). And the figure of this was indicated beforehand in the manna given in the desert. *Whoever ate of that bread were said by the Lord to have died, because remaining faithless, they did not eat of this hidden and uniquely spiritual manna by which Christ offers immortality to the faithful.* For he said, "Unless you eat the flesh of the Son of Man and drink his blood, you will not have eternal life in you" (John 6:53). For indeed, whoever at that time was able to eat spiritually, they were worthy to obtain the same immortality, as were Moses and the others. As the apostle [Paul] teaches, "They ate the same spiritual food" (1 Cor 10:3). (TYCONIUS, *COMMENTARY ON THE APOCALYPSE*, 2:17)

In this passage, Tyconius weaves together virtually every reference to the manna in the New Testament. In doing so, he reveals a very exalted view of the Christian

Eucharist: it is the hidden manna of Revelation, the flesh of the heavenly Bread "made man." Through this hidden manna, Jesus offers nothing less than immortality to those who receive it worthily.

In light of such witnesses, it is no wonder that Saint Augustine, the great African bishop theologian of the late fourth and early fifth centuries, would go on to write in his homilies on the Gospel of John:

> The manna also came down from heaven; but *the manna was a shadow, this is the truth.* "If anyone shall have eaten of this Bread, he will live forever; and the Bread which I shall give is my Flesh for the life of the world." (*TRACTATE ON JOHN*, 26:13)

For Augustine, the Eucharistic mystery was so real that he even called Christians to give to it the adoration due to God alone: "No one eats that Flesh unless he has first adored it . . . and we sin by not adoring" (*On the Psalms* 98:9).

The New Manna Today

Once again, when we turn to the contemporary teaching of the Catholic Church, we find a glowing case of continuity both with the New Testament Scriptures and the witness of the early Church Fathers.

In its discussion of the Jewish roots of Christian worship, the Catechism explicitly teaches that the manna of the exodus from Egypt pointed forward to the miraculous bread of the Last Supper. "*The manna in the desert prefigured the Eucharist,* 'the true bread from heaven'" (CCC 1094). Sure enough, in support of this teaching, the Catechism cites Jesus' bread of life sermon in the synagogue at Capernaum (John 6:32) and Saint Paul's references to the "supernatural" food and drink of the wilderness generation (1 Corinthians 10:1–6).

In fact, the Catechism even goes so far as to say that in the Lord's Prayer, when Jesus teaches his disciples to say "Give us this day our *epiousios* bread," he is teaching them to pray for the *supersubstantial* bread of the Eucharist. Although it recognizes that other meanings can be derived from Jesus' words, it has this to say about the literal meaning of the prayer:

> "Daily" (*epiousios*) occurs nowhere else in the New Testament. Taken in a temporal sense, this word is a pedagogical repetition of "this day," to confirm us in trust without reservation. Taken in the qualitative sense, it signifies what is necessary for life. . . . *Taken literally* (*epi-ousios*: "super-substantial"), *it refers directly to the Bread of Life, the Body of Christ, the "medicine of immortality" without which we have no life in us.* (CCC 2837)

I can still remember vividly the first time I read these lines. I had recently spent countless hours researching the meaning of the Greek word *epiousios*, only to arrive at the conclusion that the most literal translation was in fact "supersubstantial" (or "supernatural"). I was quite sure I had made an important "discovery," for which I would one day hopefully be rewarded with tenure (or at least thought of as brilliant). And then, by chance, while reading the Catechism's commentary on the Lord's Prayer, what do I find? My own "new" idea stated in passing as a matter of fact!

Needless to say, I never published my findings, but I

did learn a very valuable lesson: when it comes to the rich-
ness of the Christian tradition, many of its most profound
insights into the Bible have not been lost, only overlooked
by those of us who do not know them. They are there, present, just waiting to be discovered and realized anew.

In Remembrance of Me

Our third key to the secret of the Last Supper is certainly
not least: Jesus also saw the Eucharist he would institute as
the new Bread of the Presence. This final image, though
the least well known of the three, teaches us something
extremely important. It shows us that Jesus not only saw the
bread he would give to his disciples as a sign of some*thing*—
the new exodus, the new Passover, or the miracle of the
manna. He saw it as a sign of some*one*. Indeed, he saw it as
his own *personal presence*. By means of this bread, the new
Bread of the Presence, he gave the Twelve an expression
of his love for them, for the people of Israel, and for "the
many" for whom he would die on the cross (Mark 10:45).

If Jesus knew the Scriptures—and he certainly did—
then he would have known just how important the Bread of
the Presence was in the first exodus from Egypt. He would
have known that the bread was kept in the Tabernacle of
Moses, in front of the Ark of the Covenant and alongside the
golden Menorah. He would have known that it consisted of
both bread and wine, and that it was offered every week as
an unbloody Sabbath sacrifice. He would have known that
it could only be eaten by the priests, and that it was the only
sacrifice referred to in the Pentateuch as an "everlasting
covenant." He would have known that it was not just the

Bread of the Presence, but the Bread of the Face—the visible sign of God's presence, God's "face," on earth.

As a first-century Jew, Jesus also probably knew the tradition that Melchizedek—the first man to be called "priest" in the Bible—had himself offered the Bread and wine of the Presence. And he may have heard the Jewish priests in his day tell stories about how the Bread of the Presence was miraculous. But he certainly knew—since he himself had gone up to Jerusalem many times for the feasts—how the priests in the Temple would lift up the Bread of the Presence for Jewish pilgrims and cry out, "Behold, God's love for you!" He would have known that in this bread, they fulfilled their command to "see the face of the LORD" three times a year (Exodus 34:23; 23:17), and that with the Bread of the Presence they offered incense as "a remembrance" to the Lord (Leviticus 24:7).

In light of all this, it's no wonder that when Jesus wanted to leave his disciples with a visible sign of his presence, he chose bread and wine. When he wanted to leave them with a sacrifice to be offered "in remembrance" of him (1 Corinthians 11:24–25), he used the same elements that the priests in the Tabernacle of Moses had used. When he wanted to give them a sign of the "new covenant" of the new exodus—a sign of his love for them and for "the many" for whom he would die—he gave them the Bread and wine of his Presence. By doing so, he said to them and to everyone for whom he died, "Behold, God's love—behold, my love—for you."

The Bread of the Presence in Ancient Christianity

In keeping with its somewhat mysterious nature, the Bread of the Presence is mentioned only on a couple of occasions in the writings of the New Testament. One of them we already examined earlier: Jesus' debate with the Pharisees over his disciples' plucking grain on the Sabbath (Matthew 12:1–8; Mark 2:23–28; Luke 6:1–5). The other is a fleeting reference in the letter to the Hebrews, in its description of the earthly sanctuary of Moses' Tabernacle (Hebrews 9:1–3).

However, when we turn to the writings of the Church Fathers, we do find a few references to the Bread of the Presence that tie it directly to the Christian Eucharist and to the "memorial" or "remembrance" of Jesus' death that he established in the Upper Room. Yet again, Origen does not disappoint us with his insights into the Old Testament. In his commentary on the Book of Leviticus, he writes:

> The precept is given that, without ceasing, twelve loaves are placed in the sight of the Lord, so that the memory of the twelve tribes is always to be held before him. Through these things, a certain plea or supplication arises for each of the tribes. . . . But if these things are referred to the greatness of the mystery, you will find this "remembrance" to have the effect of a great propitiation. If you return to that bread "which comes down from heaven and gives life to the world" (John 6:33), that bread of the presence "whom God put forward as an expiation by his blood" (Rom 3:25), and if you turn your attention to that remembrance about which the Lord says, "Do this in remembrance of me" (1 Cor 11:25), you will find that this is the only "remembrance" that makes God gracious to men. Therefore, if you recall more intently the Church's mysteries, you will find the image of the future truth anticipated

in these things written in the law. (ORIGEN, *ON LEVITICUS* 13)

In speaking of the Church's "mysteries" (*mysterion*), Origen is using a common Greek expression for what Christians today (influenced by Latin) call the "sacraments" (*sacramentum*). In these words, he is teaching us something very important: the ceremonies and sacrifices of the Old Testament were not only the way in which God desired to be worshiped by the Israelites. They were also signs that pointed to the messianic age, "images" of the "future truth" of the mystery that Jesus would institute at the Last Supper.

In other words, for Origen, the Bread of the Presence was originally a "remembrance" of the twelve tribes of Israel. However, it was also a sign that pointed beyond itself. It was an image, instituted by God, of the future truth of what the Messiah would accomplish when he instituted the bread and wine of his own presence, commanding the Twelve disciples to offer this bread and wine "in remembrance *of me.*"

The words of Saint Cyril, the bishop of Jerusalem in the fourth century A.D., are even stronger. In his instructions for Christian initiates (known as catechumens), he uses the Old Testament Bread of the Presence to illuminate the mystery of a presence in the Eucharist that can only be called real:

> *In the Old Covenant there were the loaves of proposition [the Bread of the Presence], but they, being of the Old Covenant, have come to an end.* In the New Covenant there is a heavenly bread and a cup of salvation that sanctify soul and body. For, as the bread exists for the body, so the Word is in harmony with the soul.

> *Therefore, do not consider them as bare bread and wine; for, according to the declaration of the Master, they are Body and Blood.* If even the senses suggest this to you [viz., that they are bare bread and wine], let faith reassure you. Do not judge the reality by taste, but, having full assurance from faith, realize that you have been judged worthy of the Body and Blood of Christ. . . .
>
> Having learned these things, you have complete certitude that the visible bread is not bread, even if it is such to the taste, but the Body of Christ; and the visible wine is not wine, even if taste thinks it such, but the Blood of Christ. (CYRIL OF JERUSALEM, *MYSTAGOGIC CATECHESIS* 5–6, 9)

Could Cyril be any clearer? Here, in a nutshell, is the whole mystery of Jesus' real presence in the Eucharist. With the destruction of the Temple, the old covenant Bread of the Presence has come to an end. But now, in the Eucharist, the new bread and wine are something much greater. They are nothing less than the body and blood of the Messiah—really and truly present—under the appearances of bread and wine. For Cyril, this change is complete: after the offering of the Christian Eucharist, the visible bread of the Eucharist is no longer bread, and the visible wine is no longer wine; both have become the very body and blood of Jesus.

The Bread of the Presence Today

Unfortunately for us, the Catechism of the Catholic Church does not ever explicitly link the Old Testament Bread of the Presence to the Eucharist. The Catechism only mentions it in passing, as part of the Temple worship of the Israelite people (CCC 2581).

Nevertheless, it is significant that the Church, when explaining the mystery of the Eucharist, chooses to use the language of Jesus' real *presence*. Indeed, this teaching stands at the very heart of the Catholic faith:

> In the most blessed sacrament of the Eucharist "the body and blood, together with the soul and divinity, of our Lord Jesus Christ and therefore, the whole Christ is truly, really, and substantially contained." *This presence is called real* ... that is to say, it is a substantial presence by which Christ, God and man, makes himself wholly and entirely present. It is by the conversion of the bread and wine into Christ's body and blood that Christ becomes present in this sacrament. (CCC 1374–75)

Like Jesus, the Catholic Church teaches that the first Eucharist—and every other since—was not just a sign; it was also a miracle. It's because of this belief in the miraculous nature of the Eucharist that the Church also holds that not just anyone has the power to transform bread and wine into Jesus' body and blood, but only a validly ordained priest. And it's because of this belief in the real presence of Christ—body, blood, soul, and divinity—that the Church not only honors the Eucharist but gives to the Eucharist the worship due to God alone (CCC 1378).

In the end, however, even the Church's veneration of the Eucharist can be rooted in ancient Jewish practice and belief. Recall that at the time of Jesus, the priests in the Temple would elevate the Bread of the Presence so that the Israelites could "see" the Bread of the Face of God.

So, too, the Church now elevates and venerates the Eucharist, so that believers can contemplate the face of the Messiah, hidden under the appearances of bread and wine. Likewise, at the time of the exodus from Egypt, the Israelite priests kept the Bread of the Presence in the Tabernacle of Moses and, later, the Temple. So, too, the Catholic Church now reserves the new bread of Jesus' presence in— of all places—her many tabernacles throughout the world.

In short, by teaching the real presence of Jesus in the Eucharist, the Church is herself only restating what orthodox Christians have always believed. To be sure, going back to the beginning, there were some who claimed the name of Christian, such as the ancient Gnostics, who rejected the belief in Jesus' real presence. In about A.D. 107, Ignatius of Antioch, who was a Catholic bishop and a disciple of the apostle John, denounced anyone who called themselves Christians but did not believe in the real presence. Of the Gnostics he said:

> They abstain from Eucharist and prayer because *they refuse to acknowledge that the Eucharist is the flesh of our savior Jesus Christ*, which suffered for our sins and which the Father by his goodness raised up.
> (IGNATIUS OF ANTIOCH, *SMYRNAEANS* 6:2)

On one hand, it's amazing that in the very first generation after the apostles, the Church was already having to defend the reality of Jesus' presence in the Eucharist. How could things have gone wrong so quickly? On the other hand, however, it isn't really all that surprising, when we remember that some of Jesus' own disciples left him because of the difficulty of this teaching. The important point is this: in stark contrast to the Gnostics, the apostolic Church

Fathers and their successors not only believed in the real presence of Jesus in the Eucharist, they also recognized that it had been prefigured in the Old Testament, by means of the Passover, the manna, and the Bread of the Presence.

Therefore, if, like many people, you haven't heard much about the Jewish roots of the Eucharist before, it's not because they are something new. It's not because the New Testament writers and other ancient Christians didn't know about them. They did. And it's certainly not because no Church teaches this today. There is at least one Church that does: the Roman Catholic Church. Even when we forget, the Church remembers and it continues to proclaim the good news of the mystery of the Eucharist.

And she says even more than this. For if all of this is true—if God is really guiding salvation history from the very beginning, if Jesus really was the awaited Messiah, and the Eucharist really is his body, blood, soul, and divinity—then we can say with the Church that the Eucharist is nothing less than *"the source and the summit of the Christian life"* (CCC 1324). It is the mystery of God made man, of the Word made flesh, present to us—right now—not only in his divinity but in his humanity. In the beautiful words of Saint Thomas Aquinas's Eucharistic hymn:

> Godhead here in hiding, whom I do adore
> Masked by these bare shadows, shape and nothing more,
> See, Lord, at thy service low lies here a heart
> Lost, all lost in wonder, at the God thou art.
>
> Seeing, touching, tasting are in thee deceived;
> How says trusty hearing? That shall be believed;
> What God's Son has told me, take for truth I do.
> Truth himself speaks truly or there's nothing true.

—— ❧ ❧ ——

8

ON THE ROAD TO EMMAUS

With all of this in mind, we can end our journey by asking one final question, using one last key to the mystery of the Eucharist. The question is this: even if Jesus believed that he gave his actual body and blood to the disciples at the Last Supper, how did he think he would give it to anyone else? After all, only Twelve disciples were present in the Upper Room. But Jesus said that his blood would be poured out "for *many*" (Matthew 26:28). How did Jesus think these "many" would participate in the Eucharist?

The Jewish Hope for Resurrection

The answer may lie in Jesus' hope for the future, beyond the looming shadow of his imminent death. As the Gospels make abundantly clear, Jesus not only expected to be crucified; he also expected to be *raised from the dead*. Like many other ancient Jews, he believed in the resurrection of the body. And on several different occasions, he had taught his disciples: "The Son of man will be delivered into the hands of men, and they will kill him; and when he is killed, after three days he will rise" (Mark 9:31).

Moreover, as we saw in Chapter 4, Jesus also explicitly tied the mystery of the Eucharist to the mystery of his bodily resurrection. When his disciples murmured at the thought of eating his flesh and drinking his blood, he said to them, "Do you take offense at this? Then what if you were to see the Son of Man ascending to where he was before?" (John 6:62).

In other words, Jesus not only saw the Eucharist as a participation in his bodily *death* on the cross. He also saw it as a participation in his bodily *resurrection*. The reason he would be able to give his body and blood to "many," and not just to the disciples, is that as the messianic Son of Man, he would not just be killed, but raised, and ascend to where he was before—in heaven. There, from his heavenly throne, he would be able to pour himself out upon the altars of the world, giving his crucified *and risen* body and blood to all. Then would his promise to the apostles be fulfilled: they would be able to "eat and drink at my table in my kingdom" (Luke 22:30).

This is, I suggest, the final piece of the puzzle. This is the final key to unlocking the secrets of the Last Supper. The reason Jesus taught that it was necessary to eat his flesh and drink his blood in order to have eternal life is that he did not see eternal life as the ancient Greeks saw it. He did not see it as the mere immortality of the soul. As a first-century Jew, Jesus saw eternal life as the immortality of the soul *and the resurrection of the body*. For this reason, those who would have such life must receive it from Jesus' own body. As he says in his sermon at Capernaum, "Amen, amen, I say to you, unless you eat the flesh of the Son of Man and drink his blood, you have no life in you. He who eats my flesh and drinks my blood has *eternal life, and I will raise him up on the last day*" (John 6:53–54).

Stay with Us

After Jesus' bread of life discourse, no passage in the Gospels makes this connection between the Eucharist and the bodily resurrection better than Jesus' appearance to the disciples on the Road to Emmaus.

The story is well known. It took place on "the first day of the week" (Luke 24:1), the Sunday after Jesus' passion and death on the cross outside the walls of Jerusalem. As Luke tells us in his final chapter,

> That very day two of them were going to a village named Emmaus, about seven miles from Jerusalem, and talking with each other about all these things that had happened. While they were talking and discussing together, *Jesus himself drew near and went with them. But their eyes were kept from recognizing him.* And he said to them, "What is this conversation which you are holding with each other as you walk?" And they stood still, looking sad. Then one of them, named Cleopas, answered him, "Are you the only visitor to Jerusalem who does not know the things that have happened there in these days?" And he said to them, "What things?" And they said to him, "Concerning Jesus of Nazareth, who was a prophet mighty in deed

and word before God and all the people, and how
our chief priests and rulers delivered him up to be
condemned to death, and crucified him. But we
had hoped that he was the one to redeem Israel.
Yes, and besides all this, it is now the third day
since this happened. Moreover, some women of
our company amazed us. They were at the tomb
early in the morning and did not find his body;
and they came back saying that they had even
seen a vision of angels, who said that he was alive.
Some of those who were with us went to the tomb,
and found it just as the women had said; but him
they did not see." (LUKE 24:13–24)

Notice two things. First, readers sometimes think the
disciples just failed to recognize Jesus. But this is unlikely.
After all, it had been only three days since they last saw
him. Could they have forgotten so quickly what their master looked like? More important, that's not what Luke says.
What he says is that "their eyes were *kept* from recognizing
him." In his resurrected body, Jesus is able to appear to
them under whatever form he wishes. In his resurrected
body, Jesus can hide himself.

Second, note the state of the disciples' faith. Do they still
believe in Jesus? It doesn't seem so. Not only are they sad
because of what had happened to him, but they don't even
refer to him as the Messiah. Instead, they have demoted
Jesus to just "a prophet"—mighty in deed and word, to be
sure—but just a prophet. According to their expectations,
the Messiah was not supposed to end up dead on a Roman
cross. And even though they've heard word of the resurrection, they don't believe it. As they themselves say, "We
had hoped he was the one to redeem Israel."

So how did Jesus respond to their lack of faith? What did he do? He did exactly what we have been doing throughout this book: he went back to *the Jewish Scriptures.* He explained how they held the keys to unlocking the mystery of his passion, death, and resurrection. "Beginning with Moses and all the prophets, he interpreted to them in the Scriptures the things concerning himself" (Luke 24:25–27).

But the story doesn't end there. In fact, everything that Jesus has done so far is really just a preparation for what happens next:

> So they drew near to the village to which they were going. He appeared to be going further, but they constrained him, saying, "Stay with us, for it is toward evening and the day is now far spent." So he went in to stay with them. *When he was at table with them, he took bread and blessed and broke it, and gave it to them. And their eyes were opened and they recognized him; and he vanished out of their sight.* They said to each other, "Did not our hearts burn within us while he talked to us on the road, while he opened to us the Scriptures?" And they rose that same hour and returned to Jerusalem; and they found the Eleven gathered together and those who were with them, who said, "The Lord has risen indeed, and has appeared to Simon!" Then they told what had happened on the road, and *how he was known to them in the breaking of the bread.* (LUKE 24:28–35)

What is the meaning of this mysterious event? Why were the disciples able to recognize Jesus only after he sat at table with them and broke the bread? And why is it that as soon as they did see him, he vanished out of their sight?

The answer lies in "the breaking of the bread." Until Jesus sat down with the disciples and *repeated his actions from the Last Supper,* their eyes were kept from seeing him. Until he took the bread, blessed the bread, and broke the bread—again, exactly what he did at the Last Supper (Matthew 26:26)—they could not recognize him.

Only with the breaking of the bread was the risen Jesus made known to them. And then, as soon as they did see him, he vanished. Why? *Jesus was pointing them to the way he would be present with them from now on.* After his ascension into heaven, he would no longer be with them under the appearance of a man. From then on—with the singular exception of his appearance to Paul, on the road to Damascus—he would only be present under the appearance of the Eucharistic bread. By means of his miraculous appearance on the way to Emmaus, Jesus was showing the disciples that the Eucharist is his crucified and risen body. And in his risen body, he is no longer bound by space, or time, or even appearance. The risen Jesus can appear when he wills, where he wills, how he wills, and under whatever form he wills. He can hide himself, just as he did on the Road to Emmaus. After his resurrection and ascension into heaven, his normal manner of appearing to his disciples will not be in the form of a man, but under the veil of the Eucharist. That is why the disciples go away rejoicing in "how he was known to them in the breaking of the bread" (Luke 24:35).

In short, on the road to Emmaus, Jesus fulfilled what he set out to accomplish at the Last Supper. That Sunday was the first Eucharist after the Resurrection, and Jesus was the principal celebrant. On that day, he ate and drank with his disciples in the joy of his kingdom. On that day, he gave them his crucified and risen body and blood. And while the disciples might not have realized it at the time, on that day, Jesus answered their prayer outside the village of Emmaus, when they said to him: "*Stay with us*" (Luke 24:29). In the "breaking of the bread," in every Eucharist, he answers their prayer, saying to them—and to all of us—"I am with you always, even to the end of time."

Acknowledgments

Over five years ago, my good friend and colleague Dr. Chris Baglow, now of Notre Dame Seminary in New Orleans, invited me to speak to an audience of Catholic priests on the topic of the Eucharist. At the time, I had done a good bit of study in ancient Jewish practice and belief, but virtually none on the Eucharist. To say the least, I was somewhat daunted. What could I, as a layman, have to say to over a hundred priests who had dedicated their whole lives to the Eucharist? If I recall correctly, Chris's advice went something like this: "Don't worry. Just do something on the biblical roots of the Eucharist." It was good advice. From his suggestion was born a lecture, entitled "Jesus and the Jewish Roots of the Eucharist." Since that time, I have given this same lecture countless times, all over the United States. Remarkably, the outline is essentially the same as that which we devised all those years ago in the Benedictine Abbey library of St. Joseph Seminary College in Covington (where I now write these words). So the first debt of gratitude goes to him: Thank you, Chris, for the suggestion. It seems to have worked out well.

I am grateful to a host of other people as well: above all, to my parents, for handing on the faith to me, and for bringing me to my first Holy Communion and for always being faithful about bringing me to Mass; to my close friends and conversation partners in biblical studies, especially Michael Barber, with whom I have had countless conversations about my research in this area; to my many students at Our Lady of Holy Cross and Notre Dame Seminary, who have endured my endless lectures on the Eucharist over the years; to Brian Butler, who first gave me the idea of turning the lecture into a book that someone might actually want to read; and to all those whose willingness to pray for me and support me have helped me through a very intense five years of different jobs, different homes, and four new children!

I also want to offer thanks in a special way to Gary Jansen of Doubleday, for his enthusiasm about the project and his excellent editorial work, and to my good friend Scott Hahn, for putting me in touch with Gary and for agreeing to write the Foreword. I am deeply indebted to you both.

Last, but certainly not least, I owe anything good that is in this work to the patience, love, and support of my beautiful wife, Elizabeth, and our children: Morgen, Aidan, Hannah, Marybeth, and Baby Pitre (as yet unborn and unnamed!). Elizabeth—herself a much better writer than I am—was the first to read a draft of the manuscript. Without her guidance and support, it would be a much lesser book; without her fidelity and companionship, I would be a much lesser man. It is to her that I dedicate this work. May our family one day come together to that heavenly promised land, where even the new manna will cease, and we will no longer see the One who is the true Bread of Life through a mirror so dimly, but as He is, face to face.

NOTES

※ ⋘

INTRODUCTION

3 doctrine of Jesus' "Real Presence": See the *Catechism of the Catholic Church,* second edition (Washington, D.C.: United States Conference of Catholic Bishops, 1997), nos. 1373–78.

4 dozens of books: See, for example, Peter Kreeft and Ronald K. Tacelli, S.J., *Handbook of Catholic Apologetics: Reasoned Answers to Questions of Faith* (San Francisco: Ignatius, 2009); Scott Hahn, *Reasons to Believe: How to Understand, Explain, and Defend the Catholic Faith* (New York: Doubleday, 2007); Karl Keating, *Catholicism and Fundamentalism* (San Francisco: Ignatius, 1988).

8 Jesus had to have made sense: Amy-Jill Levine, *The Misunderstood Jew* (San Francisco: HarperCollins, 2006), 20–21.

9 [I]t must be said: Pope Benedict XVI, *Jesus, the Apostles, and the Early Church: General Audiences 15 March 2006–14 February 2007* (San Francisco: Ignatius, 2007).

1. THE MYSTERY OF THE LAST SUPPER

12 theologians have written books: In recent years, this lack of emphasis on Jesus' Jewish identity in works of Christology appears to be changing. For example, in the second revised edition of his widely used 1995 book, Gerald O'Collins adds a new chapter on the "Jewish Matrix" of Jesus' life. See Gerald

O'Collins, *Christology: A Biblical, Historical, and Systematic Study of Jesus*, second edition (Oxford: Oxford University Press, 2009), 21–43.

12 Jesus lived in an ancient *Jewish* context: In the last century or so, a host of scholarly books have focused on Jesus in his ancient Jewish context. Among Catholics, see Joseph Ratzinger (Pope Benedict XVI), *Jesus of Nazareth* (New York: Doubleday, 2007); Brant Pitre, *Jesus, the Tribulation, and the End of the Exile: Restoration Eschatology and the Origin of the Atonement* (WUNT 2.204; Tübingen, Germany: Mohr Siebeck; Grand Rapids: Baker Academic, 2005); John P. Meier, *A Marginal Jew*, 4 volumes (New York: Doubleday, 1991, 1994, 2001, 2009); and Ben F. Meyer, *The Aims of Jesus* (London: SCM Press, 1977). Among Protestants, see N. T. Wright, *Jesus and the Victory of God* (Minneapolis: Fortress, 1996); Craig A. Evans, *Jesus and His Contemporaries: Comparative Studies* (Leiden, the Netherlands: E. J. Brill, 1995); E. P. Sanders, *Jesus and Judaism* (Philadelphia: Fortress, 1985); and Joachim Jeremias, *New Testament Theology: the Proclamation of Jesus*, trans. John Bowden (London: SCM Press, 1971). Among Jewish scholars, see David Flusser (with R. Steven Notley), *The Sage from Galilee: Rediscovering Jesus' Genius* (Grand Rapids: Eerdmans, 2007); Levine, *The Misunderstood Jew*; Geza Vermes, *Jesus the Jew* (Minneapolis: Fortress, 1973); Joseph Klausner, *Jesus of Nazareth: His Life, Times, and Teaching*, trans. Herbert Danby (New York: Macmillan, 1925).

13 Jesus would utilize: Throughout this study, I will treat the four Gospels as reliable historical witnesses to the words and deeds of Jesus. In doing so, I am following the traditional Christian view of their historical reliability, as well as the official Catholic teaching promulgated in 1965 at the Second Vatican Ecumenical Council. After reaffirming the "apostolic origin" of the Gospels of Matthew, Mark, Luke, and John, Vatican II states, "Holy Mother Church has firmly and with absolute constancy maintained and continues to maintain, that *the four Gospels* just named, *whose historicity she unhesitatingly affirms, faithfully hand on what Jesus, the Son of God, while he lived among men, really did and taught* for their eternal salvation, until the day when he was taken up" (Dogmatic Constitution on Divine Revelation, *Dei Verbum* 19). See Austin Flannery, O.P., *Vatican Council II: Volume 1: The Conciliar and Postconciliar Documents*, rev. ed. (Northport, N.Y.: Costello, 1996). Because this book is aimed at a more popular audience, I will not enter into scholarly debates about the authenticity of various Gospel passages but will operate with the approach recently exemplified in Pope Benedict XVI's work *Jesus of Nazareth*. With his usual pith, Pope Benedict sums up his approach with these words: "I trust the Gospels" (p. xxi). Like Benedict, I will try to show in this study that "the Jesus of the Gospels [is] the real, 'historical' Jesus in the strict sense of the word. I am convinced, and I hope the reader will be, too, that this figure is much more logical, and historically speaking, much more intelligible than the reconstructions we have been presented with in the last decades. I believe that this Jesus—the Jesus of the Gospels—is an historically plausible and convincing figure" (p. xxii).

14 the history of Christianity: E.g., Matthew Levering, *Sacrifice and Community: Jewish Offering and Christian Eucharist* (Oxford: Blackwell, 2005); James T. O'Connor, *The Hidden Manna: A Theology of the Eucharist*, second edition (San Francisco: Ignatius, 2005); Roch Kereszty, *Wedding Feast of the Lamb: Eucharistic Theology from a Biblical, Historical, and Systematic Perspective* (Chicago: Hillenbrand, 2004); Thomas Nash, *Worthy Is the Lamb: The Biblical Roots of the Mass* (San Francisco: Ignatius, 2004); Louis Bouyer, *Eucharist: Theology and Spirituality of the Eucharistic Prayer* (Notre Dame, Ind.: University of Notre Dame Press, 1968).

16 in the ancient world: See John E. Hartley, *Leviticus*, 2 volumes (Word Biblical Commentary 4; Dallas: Word Books, 1992), 273–77.

16 explicitly breaking the biblical law: To be sure, Jesus is sometimes accused of going against the traditions of the Pharisees, such as in the case of the dispute over his disciples plucking grain on the Sabbath (Matthew 12:1–8). But there is no evidence that he ever deliberately violated the Law of Moses, and plenty of evidence that he abided by it his entire life. As he says in the Sermon on Mount: "Think not that I have come to abolish the law and the prophets; I have come not to abolish them but to fulfill them" (Matthew 5:17). See, e.g., E. P. Sanders, *Jewish Law from Jesus to the Mishnah: Five Studies* (London: SCM Press; Philadelphia: Trinity Press International, 1990), 1–90.

17 [T]he imagery of: Geza Vermes, *The Religion of Jesus the Jew* (Minneapolis: Fortress, 1993), 16.

17 I speak as: Revised Standard Version (hereafter referred to as RSV), slightly adapted.

19 With that in mind: See Craig A. Evans, *Ancient Texts for New Testament Studies: A Guide to Background Literature* (Peabody,

Mass.: Hendrickson, 2005), 173–255; Lawrence H. Schiffman, *From Text to Tradition: A History of Second Temple Judaism* (New Jersey: KTAV, 1991), 177–200, 220–239; James VanderKam and Peter Flint, *The Meaning of the Dead Sea Scrolls* (Minneapolis: Fortres, 2002); H. L. Strack and Günter Stemberger, *Introduction to the Talmud and Midrash*, trans. and ed. Markus Bockmuehl (Minneapolis: Fortress, 1996).

21 they are still very: For examples of using rabbinic literature for the study of Jesus, see Levine, *The Misunderstood Jew*; Craig A. Evans, *Jesus and His Contemporaries: Comparative Studies* (Leiden, the Netherlands: Brill, 2001); Sanders, *Jewish Law from Jesus to the Mishnah*; Vermes, *Jesus the Jew*. See also Herbert W. Basser, "The Gospels and Rabbinic Literature" in *The Missing Jesus: Rabbinic Judaism and the New Testament*, eds. Bruce Chilton, Craig A. Evans, and Jacob Neusner (Leiden, the Netherlands: Brill, 2002), 77–99.

2. WHAT WERE THE JEWISH PEOPLE WAITING FOR?

23 Chief among these: See Martin Hengel, *The Zealots* (Edinburgh: T. & T. Clark, 1961).

23 this thought does: For a nice overview of common Jewish hopes for the future, see especially E. P. Sanders, *Judaism: Practice & Belief 63BCE-66CE* (London: SCM Press; Philadelphia: Trinity Press International, 1992), 279–303; David E. Aune, *Apocalypticism, Prophecy, and Magic in Early Christianity* (WUNT 199; Tübingen, Germany: Mohr Siebeck, 2006), 13–38.

23 For if you actually: Unless otherwise noted, all translations of the Jewish Pseudepigrapha are from James H. Charlesworth, ed., *The Old Testament Pseudepigrapha*, 2 volumes; (Anchor Bible Reference Library; New York: Doubleday, 1983, 1985), and all translations of the Dead Sea Scrolls are from Florentino García Martínez and Eibert J. C. Tigchelaar, *The Dead Sea Scrolls Study Edition*, 2 volumes (Grand Rapids: Eerdmans, 2000). Translations of the Old Testament are from the Revised Standard Version, Catholic Edition (hereafter referred to as RSV). Unless otherwise noted, all English translations of the Midrash Rabbah are from H. Friedman and M. Simon, *Midrash Rabbah* (10 vols.; repr.; London: Soncino, 1992).

24 God would recapitulate: For scholarly discussions of the new exodus, see, for example, David W. Pao, *Acts and the Isaianic New Exodus* (Grand Rapids: Baker Academic, 2000); Rikki E. Watts, *Isaiah's New Exodus in Mark* (Grand Rapids: Baker Academic,

2000); Dale C. Allison, Jr., *The New Moses: A Matthean Typology* (Minneapolis: Fortress, 1993); Jean Danielou, S.J., *From Shadows to Reality: Studies in the Biblical Typology of the Fathers* (Westminster, Md.: Newman, 1960), 153–228.

27 the words of Rabbi Berekiah: There are two figures who lay claim to the title Rabbi Berekiah, one from the third and one from the fourth century A.D. See Jacob Neusner, *Dictionary of Ancient Rabbis: Selections from the Jewish Encyclopaedia* (Peabody, Mass.: Hendrickson, 2003), 100–102.

27 Rabbi Berekiah said: Translation slightly adapted from the Soncino edition of the Midrash Rabbah, which somewhat strangely reads "cornfield" for Ps 72:16. Quoted in Allison, *The New Moses*, 85.

31 Jeremiah's prophecy: Rabbi Hezekiah's identity is difficult to establish. See Neusner, *Dictionary of Ancient Rabbis*, 192. For the quotation, see *Ecclesiastes Rabbah* 2:1:1, translation slightly adapted. Compare also *Song of Songs Rabbah* 1:2–4.

32 In the World to Come: Translation Soncino Talmud (slightly adapted). For a similar adaptation, see Joseph Klausner, *The Messianic Idea in Israel*, trans. W. F. Stinesspring (London: George Allen and Unwin, 1956), 412.

32 this rabbinic tradition: Klausner, *The Messianic Idea in Israel*, 412.

32 In the new exodus: For excellent studies of the Jewish hope for a new Temple, see G. K. Beale, *The Temple and the Church's Mission: A Biblical Theology of the Dwelling Place of God* (New Studies in Biblical Theology 17; Downers Grove, Ill.: InterVarsity, 2004); T. Desmond Alexander and Simon Gathercole, eds., *Heaven on Earth: The Temple in Biblical Theology* (Waynesboro, Ga.: PaterNoster, 2004); Yves Congar, O.P., *The Mystery of the Temple* (Westminster, Md.: Newman, 1962).

33 Tabernacle of Moses: See Craig R. Koester, "Tabernacle," in *Eerdmans Dictionary of the Bible*, ed. David Noel Freedman (Grand Rapids: Eerdmans, 2000), 1269–70. For a longer study, see Craig R. Koester, *The Dwelling of God* (Catholic Biblical Quarterly Monograph Series 22; Washington, D.C.: Catholic Biblical Association, 1989).

34 Temple in Jerusalem: As N. T. Wright puts it, "The Temple was the focal point of every aspect of Jewish national life. . . . Its importance at every level can hardly be overestimated." N. T. Wright, *The New Testament and the People of God* (Minneapolis: Fortress, 1992), 224.

36 Dead Sea Scrolls: See Sanders, *Jesus and Judaism*, 77–90, for a collection of sources.

36 "bring back the worship": Although the present form of this prayer dates after the time of Jesus, there is strong evidence that the "underlying foundation of the prayer" goes back to the first century A.D., or earlier (cf. *Mishnah, Berakoth* 4:3; *Taanith* 2:2; Acts 3:1). See Emil Schürer, *The History of the Jewish People in the Age of Jesus Christ*, 3 volumes, eds. Geza Vermes, Fergus Millar, Matthew Black, and Martin Goodman (Edinburgh: T. & T. Clark, 1973–87), 2:455–63 (quotation pp. 455–56).

37 King Herod and his: See Peter Richardson, *Herod: King of the Jews and Friend of the Romans* (Minneapolis: Fortress, 1999); Ehud Netzer, *The Architecture of Herod, the Great Builder* (Grand Rapids: Baker Academic, 2008).

37 God would bring: See W. D. Davies, *The Gospel and the Land: Early Christianity and Jewish Territorial Doctrine* (Berkeley: University of California Press, 1974); Karen J. Wenell, *Jesus and Land: Sacred and Social Space in Second Temple Judaism* (London: T. & T. Clark, 2007).

38 This is the origin: On the ingathering of the lost tribes, see Pitre, *Jesus, the Tribulation, and the End of the Exile*, 31–40; Paula Fredriksen, *Jesus of Nazareth, King of the Jews* (New York: Random House, 1999), 98; Dale C. Allison, Jr., *Jesus of Nazareth: Millenarian Prophet* (Philadelphia: Fortress, 1998), 101–102, 141; Sanders, *Judaism*, 291–94; David C. Greenwood, "On Jewish Hopes for a Restored Northern Kingdom," *Zeitschrift für die alttestamentliche Wissenschaft* 88 (1976): 376–85.

39 many other such prophecies: See, e.g., Ezekiel 20:36, 41–42, and Davies, *The Gospel and the Land*, 39.

40 evidence for a hope: This being said, it is important to emphasize that I am not saying that *all* Jews saw the future land in the same way. As W. D. Davies states, "There was no *one* doctrine of the land, clearly defined and normative, but, as is usual in Judaism, a multiplicity of ideas and expectations variously and unsystematically entertained." Nevertheless, "the view that *all* Jewish eschatology was this-worldly cannot be accepted, because so many sources anticipate a transcendent order or supernatural changes 'in the end of days.'" Davies, *The Gospel and the Land*, 157 (emphasis added).

40 Unlike the earthly land: For an introduction to the *Testament of Job*, see R. P. Spitter, "Testament of Job," in James H. Charles-

worth, *Old Testament Pseudepigrapha*, 2 volumes (Anchor Bible
Reference Library; New York: Doubleday, 1983, 1985), 1:829–37.

40 *All Israelites have a share*: Unless otherwise noted, all translations of the Mishnah are from Herbert Danby, *The Mishnah*
(Oxford: Oxford University Press, 1933), 397.

41 "inheriting the land": See Davies, *The Gospel and the Land*,
123.

41 the return of the lost: The full text reads, "Our Rabbis
taught: *The ten tribes have no portion in the world to come*, as it says,
'And the Lord rooted them out of *their land* in anger, and in
wrath, and in great indignation'" (Deut 29:27). "And the Lord
rooted them out of *their land*" refers to *this world*; "and cast them
into *another land*"—to *the world to come*: this is Rabbi Akiba's
view. . . . Rabbi Simeon ben Judah said, "If their deeds are as this
day's, they will not return; otherwise they shall." Rabbi said, "*They
will enter the future world*, as it is said, '[And it shall come to pass]
in that day, that the great trumpet shall be blown, [and they shall
come which were ready to perish in the land of Assyria, and the
outcasts in the land of Egypt, and shall worship the Lord in *the
holy mount of Jerusalem*] (Isa 27:13)'" (Babylonian Talmud, *Sanhedrin*, 110b).

43 During the period: Both translations are from the Loeb
Classical Library edition of Josephus.

44 These figures, which modern scholars: See Craig S. Keener,
The Historical Jesus of the Gospels (Grand Rapids: Eerdmans,
2009), 239–41; Rebecca Gray, *Prophetic Figures in Late Second
Temple Jewish Palestine: The Evidence from Josephus* (New York:
Oxford University Press, 1993).

44 many of Jesus' words: Keener, *The Historical Jesus of the Gospels*, 238–244; Pitre, *Jesus, the Tribulation, and the End of the Exile*,
137–59, 447–51, 486–91; Dale C. Allison, Jr., "Q's New Exodus
and the Historical Jesus," in *The Sayings Source Q and the Historical Jesus*, ed. A. Lindemann (Leuven, Belgivon: Leuven University, 2001), 295–428. See also Brant Pitre, "The Lord's Prayer
and the New Exodus," *Letter & Spirit* 2 (2006): 69–96.

46 In effect, Jesus is: See Keener, *The Historical Jesus of the Gospels*, 240; Ben Witherington, *The Christology of Jesus* (Minneapolis: Fortress, 1991), 171.

46 deliberately modeling his actions: On Jesus' messianic
self-understanding and actions, see Michael F. Bird, *Are You the
One Who Is to Come? The Historical Jesus and the Messianic Question*

(Grand Rapids: Baker Academic, 2009); Keener, *The Historical Jesus of the Gospels*, 256–82; Joseph Ratzinger (Pope Benedict XVI), *Jesus of Nazareth*, 319–55; Wright, *Jesus and the Victory of God*, 477–539.

47 *exodos* **means:** See Walter Bauer, et al., *A Greek-English Lexicon of the New Testament and Other Early Christian Literature*, 2nd ed. (Chicago and London: University of Chicago Press, 1979), 276.

3. THE NEW PASSOVER

50 the shape of the Passover: For studies of the Jewish Passover, see Barry D. Smith, *Jesus' Last Passover Meal* (Lewiston, N.Y.: Edwin Mellen Press, 1993); Sanders, *Judaism*, 132–38; B. M. Bokser, *The Origins of the Seder* (Berkeley: University of California Press, 1984); J. B. Segal, *The Hebrew Passover From the Earliest Times to A.D. 70* (London: Oxford University Press, 1963); Roland de Vaux, *Ancient Israel: Its Life and Institutions* (Grand Rapids: Eerdmans, 1997), 484–92.

52 the sacrifice of the lamb: See Brant Pitre, "Jesus, the New Temple, and the New Priesthood," *Letter & Spirit* 4 (2008): 47–83.

52 there existed in Israel: See Scott W. Hahn, *Kinship by Covenant: A Canonical Approach to the Fulfillment of God's Saving Promises* (Anchor Yale Bible Reference Library; New Haven: Yale University Press, 2009), 139–42, 279, 299–300.

54 a technical term: See Francis Brown, S. R. Driver, and Charles A. Briggs, *The Brown-Driver-Briggs Hebrew and English Lexicon* (Peabody, Mass.: Hendrickson, 1996 [original 1906]), 706.

54 a branch of "hyssop": See John L. McKenzie, S.J., *Dictionary of the Bible* (New York: Touchstone, 1965), 381, citing Lev 14:4–6; Num 19:18; Ps 51:9, and Heb 9:19.

56 a "thank offering": See, e.g., Hartmut Gese, *Essays on Biblical Theology*, trans. Keith Crim (Minneapolis: Augsburg, 1981), 117–40.

59 This happens to most: For an excellent older study, see A. Z. Idelsohn, *Jewish Liturgy and Its Development* (New York: Henry Holt, 1932), 173–187.

61 Recall that Josephus: Josephus, *Life*, 1: "My family is no ignoble one, tracing its descent far back to priestly ancestors." Unless otherwise noted, all translations of Josephus contained herein are taken from the Loeb Classical Library edition, Josephus, *Works*, ed. and trans. H. St. J. Thackeray (vols. 1–5), Ralph Marcus (vols. 5–8), and Louis Feldman (vols. 9–10) (London and Cambridge: Harvard University Press, 1926–1965).

61 So these high priests: This translation is from William Whiston, *The Works of Josephus: Complete and Unabridged* (Peabody, Mass.: Hendrickson, 1987), 465.

62 Without a Temple: See George Foot Moore, *Judaism in the First Centuries of the Christian Era*, 3 volumes (Cambridge: Harvard University Press, 1927), 40; Sanders, *Judaism*, 133.

62 they are repeatedly: For the use of *rabbi*, see Matt 23:7–8; 26:25, 49; Mark 9:5; John 1:38, 49; 3:2, 26; 4:31; 6:25, etc. Synagogues are everywhere in the New Testament. See Matt 4:23; Mark 1:39; Luke 4:16, 7:5; John 6:59; Lee I. Levine, "'Common Judaism': The Contribution of the Ancient Synagogue," in *Common Judaism: Explorations in Second-Temple Judaism*, ed. Wayne O. McCready and Adele Reinhartz (Minneapolis: Fortress, 2008), 27–46.

63 As the Israeli scholar: Joseph Tabory, "The Crucifixion of the Paschal Lamb," *Jewish Quarterly Review* 86:3–4 (1996): 395–406.

63 As Tabory concludes: Tabory, "The Crucifixion of the Paschal Lamb," 395.

63 For the lamb: This translation is from Alexander Roberts and James Donaldson, *The Ante-Nicene Fathers*, 10 volumes (Peabody, Mass.: Hendrickson, 1994), 1:215.

64 At the time of Jesus: "It is certain . . . that the Passover seder itself has from very early on been imbued with an idea of remembrance that involves not just a disinterested review of bygone events but a reliving of them (see, e.g., Exod 12:14; 13:3, 9; Deut 16:3; *Jub.* 49:7; Josephus, *Ant.* 2.317)." Joel Marcus, *The Gospel According to Mark* (Anchor Yale Bible; New York: Doubleday, 2009).

65 In every generation: Translated by Danby, *The Mishnah*, 151 (slightly adapted).

66 And the chief way: Later editions of the Mishnah add, "Not our ancestors alone, but us also did He redeem with them" (Mishnah, *Peshahim* 10:5), cited in Idelsohn, *Jewish Liturgy and Its Development*, 183.

66 "In that night": I owe this to Joachim Jeremias, *The Eucharistic Words of Jesus*, trans. Norman Perrin (London: SCM Press, 1966), 206–207. Regarding Rabbi Joshua ben Hananiah, see Neusner, *Dictionary of the Ancient Rabbis*, 259–64.

67 It is a tradition: Quoted in Jeremias, *The Eucharistic Words of Jesus*, 206.

67 The Jewish passover: Jeremias, *The Eucharistic Words of Jesus*, 206–207.

68 Jesus celebrated: I should note here that many modern scholars doubt that the Last Supper was in fact a Jewish Passover meal, despite the explicit testimony of Matthew, Mark, and Luke. This doubt is primarily rooted in an apparent chronological contradiction between John's Gospel and the Synoptics. For an overview of the problem, see Jeremias, *The Eucharistic Words of Jesus*, 15–88. In a longer study on Jesus and the Last Supper still in preparation (Grand Rapids: Eerdmans, forthcoming), I will argue that the apparent contradiction is based on a misinterpretation of the word *Passover* in John's Gospel, and that all four Gospels do in fact identify the Last Supper as a Passover meal. For this solution, see e.g., Craig L. Blomberg, *The Historical Reliability of John's Gospel: Issues & Commentary* (Downers Grove, Ill.: InterVarsity, 2001), 193–94, 238–39, 246–47; Barry D. Smith, "The Chronology of the Last Supper," *Westminster Theological Journal* 53 (1991): 29–45; C. C. Torrey, "The Date of the Crucifixion According to the Fourth Gospel," *Journal of Biblical Literature* 50 (1931): 227–41; idem, "In the Fourth Gospel the Last Supper Was a Passover Meal," *Jewish Quarterly Review* 42 (1951–52): 237–50; Cornelius a Lapide, S.J., *Commentary on the Four Gospels*, 4 volumes (Fitzwilliam, N.H.: Loreto, 2008 [orig. ca. 1637]), 2:522–26; 4:512–513; Thomas Aquinas, *Summa Theologica*, Part III, Q. 46, Art. 9.

69 Second, for anyone: Joachim Jeremias actually finds fourteen parallels between the Last Supper and the Jewish Passover in *The Eucharistic Words of Jesus*, 41–62. I cite only a few of these here.

70 This fits with: See Jeremias, *The Eucharistic Words of Jesus*, 42–43, citing Deut 16:7; *Jub.* 49:16–21; *m. Pes.* 5:10; 7:12; 10:1; *t. Pes.* 6:11, etc.

73 the offering that: In the modern Jewish Seder, it is customary not to eat lamb, but the shankbone (Hebrew *z'roah*) of a lamb is part of the Passover meal in memory of the body of the lamb that was once offered in the Temple. See, e.g., Cecil Roth, ed., *The Haggadah* (London: Soncino, 1934).

73 As the great Lutheran scholar: Jeremias, *The Eucharistic Words of Jesus*, 224.

75 Christ *our Passover lamb:* Author's translation.

4. THE MANNA OF THE MESSIAH

78 In order to see: For studies of the manna, see Bruce J. Malina, *The Palestinian Manna Tradition* (Leiden, the Netherlands: Brill, 1968); R. Meyer, "*manna*," in Gerhard Kittel, ed., *Theological Dictionary of the New Testament*, 10 volumes (Grand Rapids: Eerdmans, 1967), 4:462–66.

81 The reason I even: See McKenzie, *Dictionary of the Bible*, 541.

81 To say the least: Even Josephus, who likens the manna to a natural substance that could be observed in his own day in "all that region" of the Arabian peninsula, recognizes that the impossibility of gathering more or less than one omer of manna, as well as its daily corruption, was a sign that this food was "divine and miraculous" (*Antiquities* 3:30).

81 This cannot be reconciled: See H. St. J. Thackeray, *Josephus: Jewish Antiquities Books 1–3* (Loeb Classical Library; Cambridge and London: Harvard University Press, 1930), 335 note b.

86 When we turn to the place of the manna: For an excellent summary, see Meyer, "*manna*," 4:426–66. See also Cecil Roth, "Manna," in *Encyclopedia Judaica*, 16 volumes (Jerusalem: Keter, 1971), 11: 884–885.

86 the Mishnah states: See Babylonian Talmud, *Pesahim* 54a.

87 And the Lord said: Translations from Martin McNamara, M.S.C., Robert Hayward, and Michael Maher, M.S.C., *Targum Neofiti 1: Exodus and Targum Pseudo-Jonathan: Exodus* (Collegeville, Minn.: Liturgical Press, 1994), 207–208.

88 To the contrary: See, e.g., Christopher Rowland, *The Open Heaven: A Study of Apocalyptic in Judaism and Early Christianity* (New York: Crossroad, 1982), 78–94.

88 "And God set them": I have slightly adapted the translation to eliminate the Hebrew puns, which would be of little use to English readers.

89 As the modern Jewish scholar: See the notes in the Soncino Talmud, *Hagigah* 12b.

90 We'll cite just: See also *Exodus Rabbah* 25:3 (p. 303), on how God will renew the miracle of manna in the "millennium."

90 According to the: These examples are taken from Raymond Brown, *The Gospel According to John* (Anchor Bible 29–29a; New York: Doubleday, 1966), 1:265–66; and C. H. Dodd, *The Interpretation of the Fourth Gospel* (Cambridge: Cambridge University Press, 1953), 83–84, n2, 335. See also Craig S. Keener, *The Gospel of John* (Peabody, Mass.: Hendrickson, 2003), 1:682.

91 This text: For an introduction, see A. F. J. Klijn, "2 (Syriac

Apocalypse of) Baruch," in Charlesworth, *The Old Testament Pseudepigrapha*, 1:615–620.

91 As the New Testament: Dodd, *The Interpretation of the Fourth Gospel*, 335.

93 Our Father who art: Compare Luke 11:2–4, for a shorter version of the prayer. The petition regarding the bread is present in both versions.

93 Although we could: See Pitre, "The Lord's Prayer and the New Exodus," 69–96.

94 Greek word *epiousios:* To be sure, scholars have come up with various hypothetical proposals for an original Aramaic (or Hebrew) expression. See, e.g., Meier, *A Marginal Jew*, 2:291–94. The problem with such speculation is not only the lack of manuscript evidence but also the fact that our limited knowledge of Aramaic and Hebrew as spoken at the time of Jesus makes it virtually impossible to say what Jesus could or could not have said in his mother tongue.

94 scholars continue to debate: See Walter Bauer, William F. Arndt, F. Wilbur Gingrich, and Frederick Danker, *A Greek-English Lexicon of the New Testament and Other Early Christian Literature*, 2nd ed. (Chicago and London: University of Chicago Press, 1979), 296–97; Werner Foerster, "*epiousios*," in Gerhard Kittel, ed., *Theological Dictionary of the New Testament*, 10 volumes (Grand Rapids: Eerdmans, 1967), 2:590–99.

95 strong advocates: See, for example, John Chrysostom, *The Gospel of Matthew, Homily* 19.5; cited in Manlio Simonetti, *Matthew 1–13*, 2 volumes (Ancient Christian Commentary on Scripture; Downers Grove, Ill.: InterVarsity, 2001), 1:135–36; Ephrem the Syrian, *Commentary on Tatian's Diatesseron* 6.16a, cited in Arthur A. Just, Jr., *Luke* (Ancient Christian Commentary on Scripture; Downers Grove, Ill.: InterVarsity, 2003), 187.

95 Give us this day: The actual Latin reads *Panem nostrum supersubstantialem da nobis hodie.*

95 "it is above": See Jerome, *Commentary on Matthew*, 1.6.11; cited in Simonetti, *Matthew 1–13*, 135.

95–96 Saint Cyprian of Carthage: See Cyprian, *Treatises* 4.18; cited in Simonetti, *Matthew*, 135; see also Roberts and Donaldson, *Ante-Nicene Fathers*, 5:452, and John Cassian, *Conference* 9.21, cited in Just, *Luke*, 187; Cyril of Jerusalem, *Mystagogic Lectures*, 23.15, in Philip Schaff and Henry Wace, *Nicene and Post-Nicene Fathers: Second Series*, 14 volumes (Peabody, Mass.: Hendrickson, 1994), 7:155.

97 Manna was not needed: N. T. Wright, "The Lord's Prayer as a Paradigm for Christian Prayer," in *Into God's Presence: Prayer in the New Testament*, ed. Richard N. Longenecker (Grand Rapids: Eerdmans, 2001), 132–54 (here 143).

97 It should go: This last paragraph is adapted from Pitre, "The Lord's Prayer and the New Exodus," 87.

100 [Jesus said:]: Translation here is the RSVCE, slightly adapted. See Brown, *The Gospel According to John*, 282–83.

101 Jesus is speaking: See Rudolf Schnackenburg, *The Gospel According to St. John: Volume 2* (New York: Crossroad, 1990), 56–78.

101 striking parallels: See Jeremias, *The Eucharistic Words of Jesus*, 108.

101 any attempt to insist: Take, for example, the unconvincing attempt to dissociate John 6 from the Last Supper in the otherwise excellent book by Craig Blomberg *The Historical Reliability of John's Gospel* (Downers Grove, Ill.: InterVarsity, 2001), 126–27.

103 Old Testament prefigurations: On biblical typology, see Danielou, *From Shadows to Reality*; Leonhard Goppelt, *Typos: The Typological Interpretation of the Old Testament in the New*, trans. Donald Madvig (Grand Rapids: Eerdmans, 1982).

107 Again, Jesus' Eucharistic: Compare Mark 4:1–20.

109 to echo the famous: Lewis's words are: "I am trying here to prevent anyone saying the really foolish thing that people often say about Him: 'I'm ready to accept Jesus as a great moral teacher, but I don't accept his claim to be God.' That is the one thing we must not say. A man who was merely a man and said the sort of things Jesus said would not be a great moral teacher. He would either be a lunatic—on a level with the man who says he is a poached egg—or else he would be the Devil of Hell. You must make your choice. Either this man was, and is, the Son of God; or else a madman or something worse. You can shut Him up for a fool, you can spit at Him and kill Him as a demon; or you can fall at His feet and call him Lord and God. But let us not come with any patronizing nonsense about His being a great human teacher. He has not left that option open to us. He did not intend to." C. S. Lewis, *Mere Christianity* (London: Collins; New York: Macmillan, 1955), 52.

109 mystery of his divine: On Jesus' divine identity, see Ratzinger, *Jesus of Nazareth*, 319–355; Dean L. Overman, *A Case for the Divinity of Jesus: Examining the Earliest Evidence* (New York: Rowman & Littlefield, 2010); Beverly Roberts Gaventa and Richard B. Hays, eds., *Seeking the Identity of Jesus: A Pilgrimage* (Grand Rapids: Eerdmans, 2008); and Richard Bauckham, *Jesus and the God of Israel* (Grand Rapids: Eerdmans, 2008). In my opinion, Hilarin Felder, O.F.M. Cap., *Christ and the Critics*, 2 volumes; trans. John L. Stoddard (London: Burns Oates and Washbourne, 1924), although somewhat dated and virtually forgotten, remains the most brilliant and exhaustive modern examination of the biblical evidence for Jesus' divine self-understanding.

112 New Testament scholar: Brown, *The Gospel of John*, 1:303.

112 This idea goes back: Zwingli's exact words are, "Now I want no one to suffer himself to be offended by this painstaking examination of words; for it is not upon them that I rely, but upon the one expression 'The flesh profiteth nothing' (Jn 6:63). This expression is strong enough to prove that 'is' in this passage is used for 'signifies' or 'is a symbol of,' even if the discourse itself contained absolutely nothing by which the meaning here could be detected. . . . I have now refuted, I hope, this senseless notion about bodily flesh." Ulrich Zwingli, *Commentary on True and False Religion*, ed. S. M. Jackson (Durham: Labyrinth Press, 1981), 231 and 216, cited in O'Connor, *The Hidden Manna*, 144. Notice that Zwingli is not interested in any "painstaking examination" of the actual context of Jesus' words. There is no discussion of the whole sermon and certainly no mention of the Eucharist as the new manna. He takes one verse—John 6:63—entirely out of context, and treats it as if it alone were conclusive evidence Jesus is saying that the Eucharist is only "a symbol of" his body. This is a classic example of a text, taken out of context, being used as a pretext.

113 In Greek, the word: See the article on "spirit" (*pneuma*) in Bauer et al., *A Greek-English Lexicon of the New Testament*, 674–78. It should also be noted that Jesus does not say his words are "spiritual" (*pneumatikos*), although even this word is not defined as "metaphorical."

113 He did *not* say: St. John Chrysostom pointed this out a long time ago: "It was carnal to doubt how our Lord could give His flesh to eat. What then? Is it not real flesh? Yea, verily. In saying then that *the flesh profiteth nothing*, He does not speak of His own flesh, but that of the carnal hearer of his word." Cited in Thomas Aquinas, *Catena Aurea Volume IV–Part I: St. John* (London: John Henry Parker, 1842), 248. Augustine also wrestled with the question in his *Tractates on John* 27.5. See O'Connor, *The Hidden Manna*, 68.

113 In light of: E.g., James Dunn, who argues that John 6:63 means that "The *eucharistic* flesh avails nothing; life comes through the Spirit and words of Jesus." James D. G. Dunn, *Baptism in the Holy Spirit: A Re-examination of the New Testament Teaching on the Gift of the Spirit in Relation to Pentecostalism Today* (SBT 2.15; London: SCM Press, 1970), 184–85.

113–14 People who make this: Saint Augustine pointed this out centuries ago when he wrote "Therefore, why do you say, 'The Flesh profits nothing'? It profits nothing as they understood it: for they understood the flesh as it is when cut up in a corpse or sold in meat market, not as it is when animated by spirit. . . . And so in this case where it is said, 'Flesh profits nothing.' It refers to flesh by itself. Let spirit be added to flesh—as charity is added to knowledge—and the flesh profits very much. For, if flesh profited nothing, the Word would not have become Flesh so that he might dwell among us." Augustine, *Tractatus in Jo.* 27:5; translation in O'Connor, *The Hidden Manna*, 68.

114 By speaking of *"the* flesh": See Bauer, *A Greek-English Lexicon*, 744, and Brown, *The Gospel According to John*, 1.131: "For John, 'flesh' emphasizes the weakness and mortality of the creature. . . . Spirit, as opposed to flesh, is the principle of divine power and life operating in the human sphere."

114 They didn't understand: In a similar way, when Peter proclaimed Jesus to be the Messiah, "the son of the living God," Jesus said to him: "flesh [*sarx*] and blood has not revealed this to you, but my Father in heaven" (Matt 16:17). By means of God's grace, Peter was able to see beyond the mere appearance of Jesus' humanity to his divine sonship.

114 "He who serves": For a slightly different translation, see Freedman and Simon, *Midrash Rabbah*, 2:758, 168.

5. THE BREAD OF THE PRESENCE

117 Rabbi Menahem of Galilee: See W. D. Davies, *Torah in the Messianic Age and/or the Age to Come* (SBLMS 7; Philadelphia: Society of Biblical Literature, 1952), 55–56; Hartmut Gese, "The Origin of the Lord's Supper," in *Essays on Biblical Theology*, trans. Keith Crim (Minneapolis: Augsburg, 1981), 117–140 (here 130).

118 In order to see: See Paul V. M. Flesher, "Bread of the Presence," in *Anchor Bible Dictionary*, 6 volumes, ed. David Noel Freedman et al. (New York: Doubleday, 1992), 1:780–81; Menahem Haran, "Shewbread," *Encyclopedia Judaica*, 16 volumes, ed. Cecil Roth (Jerusalem: Keter, 1971), 14:1394–96; Jeremias, *The Eucharistic Words of Jesus*, 63–65.

118 Despite most readers': See Exod 25:23–30; 37:10–16; Lev 24:5–9; Num 4:7; 1 Sam 21:5–7; 1 Kgs 7:48; 1 Chron 9:32; 23:29; 28:16; 2 Chron 2:4; 13:11; 29:18; Neh 10:33; 1 Mac 1:22; 4:49; Matt 12:4; Mark 2:26; Luke 6:4; Heb 9:2.

120 Instead, this wine: See Menahem Haran, *Temples and Temple-Service in Ancient Israel* (Oxford: Clarendon, 1978), 216–17.

120 However, the actual Hebrew: Strangely enough, it is Catholic translations that translate the phrase as "bread of continual offering" (Jerusalem Bible) or "showbread" (New American Bible), whereas Protestant or ecumenical translations render it literally as "bread of the Presence" (Revised Standard Version; New International Version), as do Jewish commentators such as Umberto Cassuto, *A Commentary on the Book of Exodus*, trans. Israel Abrahams (Jerusalem: Magness, 1967), 340. The unfortunate term *showbread* or *shewbread* appears to have passed over into English by way of the old German *Schaubrod*, which is a translation of the Latin Vulgate's "bread of proposition" (*panes propositionis*). This comes from the occasions on which the Bread of the Presence is referred to as "the bread of laying out" or "bread of the row" (1 Chron 9:32; 23:29; Neh 10:34; Heb 9:2).

120 some scholars translate: E.g., Cassuto, *A Commentary on the Book of Exodus*, 340; Baruch A. Levine, *Leviticus* (The JPS Torah Commentary; Philadelphia: Jewish Publication Society, 1989), 165, translating it as "bread of display."

121 It tells us: For criticisms of this interpretation, see P. A. H. De Boer, "An Aspect of Sacrifice," in *Studies in the Religion of Ancient Israel*, ed. G. W. Anderson et al. (Vetus Testamentum Supplements; Leiden, the Netherlands: Brill, 1972), 27–47. As he points out, translating the Hebrew expression as "bread of display" (JPS) tells us "what should be done with the cakes, but does not translate *hapanim*" (32).

121 the meaning of: See, e.g., John E. Hartley, *Leviticus* (Word Biblical Commentary 4; Dallas: Word Books, 1991), 400: "The Hebrew literally means 'bread of the face' or 'facial bread.'" See also de Vaux, *Ancient Israel*, 422: "Rather similar to the offerings just described is the shewbread, called in Hebrew *lehem happanim* ['the bread of the face' (of God)], or 'the bread of the Presence' . . ."; De Boer, "An Aspect of Sacrifice," 34. This seems to me to be the strongest position, especially since recent research shows that in the ancient world, cakes of bread that were offered as sacrificed in temples (and later churches) would often have a symbol of the deity stamped onto them (compare Jeremiah 7:18; 44:19). See George Galavaris, *Bread and the Liturgy: The Symbolism of Early Christian and Byzantine Bread Stamps* (Madison: University of Wisconsin Press, 1970), 22.

122 As one Old Testament scholar: De Boer, "An Aspect of Sacrifice," 35.

122 And you shall take: RSVCE, slightly adapted.

124 two kinds of sacrifice: See George Buchanan Gray, *Sacrifice in the Old Testament: Its Theory and Practice* (New York: KTAV, 1971 [original 1925]), 398–402.

124 In the Old Testament, incense: De Vaux, *Ancient Israel*, 422.

127 Moreover, as the first-century: See Hahn, *Kinship by Covenant*, 97–100, 130–34; Martin McNamara, "Melchizedek: Gen 14, 17–20 in the Targums, in Rabbinic and Early Christian Literature," *Biblica* 81 (2000): 1–31; L. Ginzberg, *Legends of the Jews*, 7 volumes (Philadelphia: Jewish Publication Society, 1968), 5:225–26.

127 At that time, all: It is interesting to note that some of these traditions, including the one cited above, also connect the Bread of the Presence with the banquet of "lady Wisdom" described in Proverbs 9:1–4. E.g., *Leviticus Rabbah* 11:4 ("She has mingled her wine," refers to the drink-offerings. "She has also set her table" alludes to the setting out of the loaves of shewbread."); *Numbers Rabbah* 13:15–16 ("'Come, eat of my bread' [Prov 9:5], and in connection with the shewbread it says, 'And you shall make the dishes thereof, and the bowls thereof' [Exod 25:29]; and we learned that 'the dishes thereof' were the moulds, the shewbread having been prepared in moulds."). In a similar vein, G. K. Beale cites a tradition that the Bread of the Presence "would appear to reflect the food produced in the Garden for Adam's sustenance." See Beale, *The Temple*, 74–75.

128 These horns: According to Herbert Danby, there were "small pieces of dough put on the four upper corners after the manner of the horns of the altar." Danby, *The Mishnah*, 507 n10.

128 In the Porch: Translation slightly adapted. See Danby, *The Mishnah*, 508–509, and Mishnah *Shekalim* 6:4.

130 They would remove: See also Babylonian Talmud, *Hagigah* 26b: "It teaches, therefore, that they used to lift it and show thereon to the Festival pilgrims the showbread, and say to them,

Behold the love in which you are held by the Omnipresent." See also Mishnah, *Sukkoth* 5:7; *Menahoth* 11:4.

132 It seems to me: Israel Knohl, "Post-Biblical Sectarianism and the Priestly Schools," *Tarbiz* 60 (1991): 140–41, cited by Gary A. Anderson, "To See Where God Dwells: The Tabernacle, the Temple, and the Origins of the Christian Mystical Tradition," *Letter & Spirit* 5 (2008): 13–45 (here 25).

134 Even though the Old: For the Jewish sources, see W. D. Davies and Dale C. Allison, Jr., *A Critical and Exegetical Commentary on the Gospel According to Saint Matthew*, 3 volumes (London: T. & T. Clark, 1988, 1991, 1998), 2:307–311; Meier, *A Marginal Jew*, 4:235–51, 267–93.

134 At that time Jesus: Compare Mark 2:23–28; Luke 6:1–5.

136 the regular practice: Compare Exod 19:15; Lev 15:16–18; Deut 23:10–11; see also 11QTemple [11Q19] 45:7–12.

137 According to the Bible, David: See Hahn, *Kinship by Covenant*, 180–82, 192–93, 198–200; C. E. Armending, "Were David's Sons Priests?" in *Current issues in Biblical and Patristic Interpretation*, ed. G. Hawthorne (Grand Rapids: Eerdmans, 1975), 75–86; A. Cody, *A History of Old Testament Priesthood* (Rome: Pontifical Biblical Institute, 1969), 105.

138 Bread and wine: See Crispin H. T. Fletcher-Louis, "Jesus as the High-Priestly Messiah: Part 2," *Journal for the Study of the Historical Jesus* 5 (2007): 57–79 (esp. 76).

140 "tabernacling": See Brant Pitre, "Jesus, the New Temple, and the New Priesthood," in *Letter & Spirit* 4 (2008): 47–83 (here 53).

146 In the Old Testament also: Translation in Philip Schaff and Henry Wace, *Nicene and Post-Nicene Fathers: Second Series*, 14 volumes (Peabody, Mass.: Hendrickson, 1994), 7:152 (slightly adapted).

146 As Cyril says: See Cyril of Jerusalem, *Mystagogical Catechesis*, 4:2; in Schaff and Wace, *Nicene and Post-Nicene Fathers, Second Series*, 7:151; O'Connor, *The Hidden Manna*, 27–31.

6. THE FOURTH CUP AND THE DEATH OF JESUS

149 the Hebrew word: For translations of the Tosefta, see Jacob Neusner, *The Tosefta*, 2 volumes (Peabody, Mass.: Hendrickson, 2002).

149 By studying the striking: For reconstructions similar to that which I propose here, see Jeremias, *The Eucharistic Words of Jesus*, 85–86; Scot McKnight, *Jesus and His Death: Historiography, the*

Historical Jesus, and Atonement Theory (Waco: Baylor University Press, 2005), 256; and I. Howard Marshall, *Last Supper and Lord's Supper* (Grand Rapids: Eerdmans, 1981), Table 1.

151 the Passover meal itself: For what follows, see Mishnah, *Pesahim* 10:1–2.

151 the cup of sanctification: Mishnah, *Pesahim* 10:2.

152 "Blessed are you": The text of the Mishnah itself quotes this in an abbreviated form, but the standard blessing is meant to fill in the gap. See Jacob Neusner, *The Mishnah: A New Translation* (New Haven and London: Yale University Press, 1988), 9.

152 the cup of proclamation: Mishnah, *Pesahim* 10:4.

154 "And you shall tell": I have slightly modified Herbert Danby's translation.

155 It would signal: See Mishnah, *Pesahim* 10:7; Tosefta, *Pisha* 10:9.

155 This morsel is referred: See the reference to the *parpereth* in some manuscripts of Mishnah, *Pesahim,* 10:3; cf. Mishnah, *Berakoth* 3:5; *Aboth* 3:19; Danby, *The Mishnah,* 150 n5.

156 First, the remaining portion: Mishnah, *Pesahim* 10:7.

159 "cup of blessing": "Jesus now takes what was probably the Passover's third cup, after the main course." Darrell L. Bock, *Luke,* 2 volumes (Grand Rapids: Baker, 1996), 2:1727. "Acc[ording] to the account in Lk. the eschatological sayings is related to the first Passover cup. . . . The Jewish cup of blessing (*kol shel berakah*) corresponds to the cup of the interpretive saying (Mk. 14.23 par. Mt. 26:27; 1 C. 11:25; Lk. 22:20)." Leonhard Goppelt, *"poterion," Theological Dictionary of the New Testament,* 10 volumes, ed. G. Kittel (Grand Rapids: Eerdmans, 1968), 6:153–54. "Within the passover context, the cup mentioned in verse 17" is "the third cup, the so-called cup of blessing." G. R. Beasley-Murray, *Jesus and the Kingdom of God* (Grand Rapids: Eerdmans, 1985), 261. Beasley-Murray is following H. Schürmann, *Der Einsetzungsbericht Lk. 22, 19–20* (Münster, Germany: Aschendorff, 1955), 133–50.

160 "cup of proclamation": See, e.g., Joseph A. Fitzmyer, *The Gospel According to Luke* (2 vols.; Anchor Bible; New York: Doubleday, 1983, 1985). It should be noted that some scholars think it was the first cup. E.g., Beasley-Murray, *Jesus and the Kingdom of God,* 262.

160 But instead of referring: "Jesus reinterprets elements of the Passover meal in terms of himself. His words over the bread and 'the cup after the meal' are to be understood as a reinterpretation of the declaration of the *paterfamilias* over the bread taken at the meal proper, 'This is "the bread of affliction"' (Exod 16:3), which our fathers had to eat as they came out of Egypt. . . . Instead of identifying the unleavened *massot* as 'the bread of affliction,' Jesus identifies the bread with his 'body,' i.e., with himself." Fitzmyer, *The Gospel According to Luke*, 2:1391.

161 As most commentators: "When the Second Temple was standing, the scriptural portion known as the Hallel ('Praise'), which consists of Psalms 113–18, was sung there at Passover (cf. *m. Pes.* 5:7), as it was at Tabernacles, Hannukah, and Weeks. Probably already in Second Temple times Jews began singing the Hallel at the conclusion of the Passover seder as well." Marcus, *The Gospel According to Mark*, 2:968. See also Davies and Allison, *Saint Matthew*, 3:483–84; Bokser, *Origins of the Seder*, 43–45.

162 There is . . . in Matthew: David Daube, *The New Testament and Rabbinic Judaism* (Peabody, Mass.: Hendrickson, 1995 [original 1956]), 330–31.

165 The cup from: Lane, *The Gospel According to Mark*, 508. See also Gillian Feeley-Harnick, *The Lord's Table: Eucharist and Passover in Early Christianity* (Philadelphia: University of Pennsylvania Press, 1981), 145. Numerous scholars have recognized the multiple cups of the Last Supper as the second and third cups of the Jewish Passover, although not all of them trace out the implications of Jesus' vow for the fourth cup. E.g., Beasley-Murray, *Jesus and the Kingdom of God*, 262-63; Fitzmyer, *The Gospel According to Luke*, 2:1390; Hermann Patsch, *Abendmahl und historischer Jesus* (Stuttgart, Germany: Calwer, 1972), 90–100.

167 "took a sponge": Author's translation. English translations of this passage sometimes give the false impression that the bystander offered Jesus only wine to drink, and that perhaps he didn't drink it. Not only does the Gospel of John make clear that he did, but in Matt 27:48 and Mark 15:36, the Greek word *potizo* is a causative form, meaning that he "caused" Jesus to drink it. Whenever they "offered" Jesus wine to drink but he did not drink it, Matthew used a different Greek verb; he says that they "gave him to drink" (*edokan auto piein*) (Matthew 27:34).

167 After this Jesus: RSVCE, slightly adapted. I have translated the Greek word *oxos* literally as "sour wine" rather than as the RSV's "vinegar," which is somewhat misleading for English readers.

170 Interpreting in advance: A.E.J. Rawlinson, "Corpus Christi," in *Mysterium Christi*, eds. G. K. A. Bell and A. Deissman (London: Longmans, Green and Co., 1930), 241, cited in Beasley-Murray, *Jesus and the Kingdom of God*, 258. The same point is made by Albert Vanhoye, S.J., *Old Testament Priests and the New Priest*, trans. J. Bernard Orchard, O.S.B. (Petersham, Mass.: St. Bede's, 1986), 50, 53–54.

7. THE JEWISH ROOTS OF THE CHRISTIAN FAITH

173 Jesus had probably: See Martin Hengel, *Crucifixion* (Philadelphia: Fortress, 1977).

175 This strongly suggests: See Scott Hahn, *The Lamb's Supper: The Mass as Heaven on Earth* (New York: Doubleday, 1998).

176 "The mystery": Translation in St. Justin Martyr, *Dialogue with Trypho*, trans. Thomas B. Falls, ed. Michael Slusser (Washington, D.C.: Catholic University of America Press, 2003), 61–62.

176 Some object that: Quoted in Aquilina, *The Mass of the Early Christians*, 153.

177 These teachings are: *Catechism of the Catholic Church*, second edition (Washington, D.C.: United States Conference of Catholic Bishops, 1997).

182 It also anticipated: See Graham H. Twelftree, *Jesus the Miracle Worker* (Downers Grove, Ill.: InterVarsity, 1999), 319; W. D. Davies and Dale C. Allison, Jr., *A Critical and Exegetical Commentary on the Gospel According to Saint Matthew*, 3 volumes (Edinburgh: T. & T. Clark, 1988, 1991, 1997), 2:418.

183–84 Although commentators continue: See Michael Barber, *Coming Soon: Unlocking the Book of Revelation* (Steubenville, Ohio: Emmaus Road, 2005), 65; David E. Aune, *Revelation*, 3 volumes (Word Biblical Commentary 52; Dallas: Word Books, 1997), 189.

185 "Then, in likeness": Cited in Aquilina, *The Mass of the Early Christians*, 147–48.

185 "To him who conquers": Translation in William C. Weinrich, *Revelation* (Ancient Christian Commentary on Scripture, New Testament XII; Downers Grove, Ill.: InterVarsity, 2005), 31–32.

186 The manna also came: Translation in O'Connor, *The Hidden Manna*, 65.

186 For Augustine: Translation in O'Connor, *The Hidden Manna*, 58.

187 "Daily" (*epiousios*) occurs: Although the official English translation of the Catechism has the word *super-essential* here, the original Latin translates *epiousios* literally as "super-substantiale," in accord with the ancient Church Fathers and the position I argued for above. See *Catechismus Catholicae Ecclesiae* (Città de Vaticano: Libreria Editrice Vaticana, 1997), 714.

190 The precept is: Cited in Aquilina, *The Mass of the Early Christians*, 151–52.

191 *In the Old Covenant:* Translation in O'Connor, *The Hidden Manna*, 28.

192 For Cyril: According to the great patristic scholar Johannes Quaesten, for Cyril, "this Real Presence is brought about by a changing of the substance of the elements, and thus he is the first theologian to interpret this transformation in the sense of transubstantiation." See Johannes Quaesten, *Patrology*, 3 volumes (Westminster, Md.: Newman, 1960), 3:375. Quoted in O'Connor, *The Hidden Manna*, 30 n49.

194 So, too, the Catholic Church: Compare CCC 1378–79.

194 They abstain from: Translated by Michael W. Holmes, *The Apostolic Fathers: Greek Texts and English Translations*, 3rd ed. (Grand Rapids: Baker Academic, 2007), 255.

195 Godhead here in hiding: St. Thomas Aquinas, *Adoro te devote*, trans. by Gerard Manley Hopkins; cited in the *Catechism of the Catholic Church*, no. 1381.

8. ON THE ROAD TO EMMAUS

197 Like many other ancient: This has been fully documented in the excellent work by N. T. Wright *The Resurrection of the Son of God* (Christian Origins and the Question of God 3; Minneapolis: Fortress, 2003).